Advance praise for

CONFESSIONS OF A FAIRY'S DAUGHTER

"With **great skill and tenderness and a gorgeously wicked sense of humor**, Alison Wearing tells her family's story from every angle, allowing all to speak with their own voices. This is **an important historical document**—a portrait of gay life in the 1980s with its bravely fought battles for equality—that doesn't flinch from showing the collateral damage of homophobia, which still today affects and afflicts the families of so many who are struggling to come out. But it's also **a timeless memoir written by a loving daughter who is finding her own way in the world and learning about the need we all have not just for acceptance, but for true understanding**."

Will Schwalbe, author of *The End of Your Life Book Club*

"*Confessions of a Fairy's Daughter* had me in tears: first of laughter, then of sadness, then of wonder at life's strange and marvelous fragility. It is a book both beautiful and true; about the longing for family and for home. **Alison Wearing is a hugely talented writer**."

Alison Pick, author of *Far to Go*,
longlisted for the Man Booker Prize

"This **exquisitely written and deeply compassionate** memoir tells the story of a family and a nation at a turning point in their sexual and political awakening. The scope of events and emotions may be operatic, but Alison Wearing captures them all in details that are intimate yet revealing, heartbreaking yet joyous. **This is a book for every daughter who loves her father and for everyone who chooses to live (and love) openly and freely**."

Kamal Al-Solaylee, author of *Intolerable: A Memoir of Extremes*,
finalist for the Hilary Weston Writers' Trust Prize for Nonfiction

"Alison Wearing is blessed with **the eye of a lyric poet, the ear of a comic novelist, and a heart capacious enough to tell a complicated love story.** *Confessions of a Fairy's Daughter* caught me from the beginning and held me until its touching conclusion."

Katherine Ashenburg, author of *The Dirt on Clean* and *The Mourner's Dance*

"Part memoir, part history book, part diary and **all parts heart**. Alison Wearing weaves a tale that celebrates the complexities of who we are and the families we hold close. *Confessions of a Fairy's Daughter* is **painful, tender, poignant and—most important— beautifully honest.**"

Brian Francis, author of *Natural Order*

"*Confessions of a Fairy's Daughter* is **a universally appealing memoir** about everything that matters in a family and to a person. It will appeal to you if you have a gay parent or a straight parent or any parent. If you have a child or were once a child. If you are passionately interested in social history or all you really want is **a compelling, beautifully written story with just the right mix of everything**—compassion, discovery, recovery, the occasional (OK, on one occasion) accidental ingestion of hallucinogens on Christmas Day, music, humour, grace."

Jamie Zeppa, author of *Every Time We Say Goodbye* and *Beyond the Sky and the Earth*

CONFESSIONS
of a
FAIRY'S DAUGHTER

CONFESSIONS
of a
FAIRY'S
DAUGHTER

GROWING UP WITH A GAY DAD

ALISON WEARING

Alfred A. Knopf Canada

PUBLISHED BY ALFRED A. KNOPF CANADA

Copyright © 2013 Alison Wearing

All rights reserved under International and Pan-American Copyright
Conventions. No part of this book may be reproduced in any form or by any
electronic or mechanical means, including information storage and retrieval
systems, without permission in writing from the publisher, except by a reviewer,
who may quote brief passages in a review. Published in 2013 by Alfred A. Knopf
Canada, a division of Random House of Canada Limited, Toronto. Distributed in
Canada by Random House of Canada Limited.

www.randomhouse.ca

Knopf Canada and colophon are registered trademarks.

Library and Archives Canada Cataloguing in Publication

Wearing, Alison, 1967–
Confessions of a fairy's daughter : growing up with a gay dad / Alison Wearing.

Issued also in an electronic format.

ISBN 978-0-345-80757-1

1. Wearing, Alison, 1967–. 2. Wearing, Joe. 3. Children of gay parents—
Canada—Biography. 4. Gay fathers—Canada—Biography. 5. Fathers and
daughters. I. Title.

HQ777.8.W43 2013   306.874'208664   C2012-907990-1

Text and cover design by Kelly Hill

Images: Courtesy of the author

Printed and bound in the United States of America

2 4 6 8 9 7 5 3 1

for my father

because my father lived his soul
love is the whole and more than all

ee cummings

CONTENTS

Prelude

Partway through the writing of this book, I called my father to ask if he and I could have a cup of tea together and talk about a few things.

"Sure, that would be terrific!" he replied, his voice bouncing with enthusiasm, so I travelled into Toronto a few days later with a notebook in my bag.

My dad knew I was writing a book about growing up with a gay father. I had sent him early drafts of the first chapters, and while he had squirmed initially, asking if I wouldn't mind waiting until he had gone dotty before I published anything, he agreed that it was indeed an important story and would do well to be out in the world.

He just wished it didn't have to focus so much on *him*.

I arranged for us to talk because I had reached a bit of an impasse, having written all the scenes that I knew were important to telling my side of the story and feeling the need to broaden the narrative's perspective. I knew little about my father's early adulthood, except what one gleans from passing mentions of university days and commentary on old photos, so I had questions about that period of his life. And I knew that he had come out during the vanguard of the gay revolution in Canada and I wondered if tying his story into that cultural and political history would give the book the wider vision I was seeking.

So we had tea. Earl Grey, I believe, with milk. And toast with Marmite. Between sips and bites, I asked him about his childhood—*when did he first have the hots for a boy?*—about his years at university—*did his time at Oxford, the stomping grounds of Oscar Wilde (among others), give him the freedom to consider the possibility that he might be gay?*—and about the gay revolution in Canada—*was he at the famous Toronto bathhouse raids protest and what was it like?* We talked for hours, our conversation spilling over into all sorts of other topics along the way. I made a few pages of notes.

"Ultimately, this is *your* story, Dad," I said towards the end. "So is there anything else that *you* feel would be important to include?"

My father mentioned a few books I might read—academic treatises on gay social and political movements, the odd novel—and I jotted them down. Then he looked away pensively, inhaled sharply and opened his mouth, as if to add something. But instead of speaking, he simply held both posture and breath. Without explanation, he then got up and disappeared to his basement, reappearing a few minutes later with a small box, which he placed on the kitchen table.

"You might want to look through this," he said, and walked over to the counter to begin preparing dinner.

I asked the obvious.

"Oh, just a few papers," he replied. Casual as could be.

I peered inside: newspapers, magazine clippings, notebooks and loose papers. The first page I pulled out was filled with my father's inimitable scrawl. It was a diary entry dated January 31, 1980. I read the opening sentence aloud: "'Last night I made it with a Roman Catholic priest.'"

My dad shrieked and turned around. But instead of running over and tearing the page from my hands, he melted into a coy posture and cooed, "Oooh, I remember him. He was *so* cute . . ." Then he giggled and returned to the task of making dinner. Duck à l'orange.

I looked back at the collection of yellowing pages and realized what it was: a writer's dream. The Mythical Box, the treasure trove containing priceless original documents, the journals, the letters, clues and confessions. Everything necessary to inspire and inform a literary portrait.

Or, in this case, finish one.

After years of denial, introspection, reluctant suspicions and eventual surrender, my father came out in the 1980s. While it was difficult for a plethora of reasons, stepping into the truth of who he was brought with it such immense relief that my father must have flung the proverbial closet door right off its hinges, for he went from living a life of secrets and (for a time) deceptions to being open, forthcoming and exuberantly transparent about everything.

So while it was well within his character to share personal details, it was still a bit of a shock to be handed his diaries. Doubly extraordinary, however, was that he chose to share everything with me knowing that I was writing a memoir—one that he already wished did not have to focus so much on *him*.

At my father's kitchen table I began to sift through the papers: drafts of letters he had written to friends in the early days of his coming out, letters he had received, newspaper clippings about "Faggots as Fathers," his diaries, and various drafts—furiously handwritten, then typed on a manual typewriter, then on an electric one—of something he called "My Story," his attempts to understand and articulate what he was discovering about himself, who he had been, and who, to his combined relief, distress and amazement, he was becoming.

As my dad julienned orange peels and trussed the duck and I sifted through the treasures in The Box, I asked him the odd question—"Who was Tom? You sure wrote a lot about him . . ."—and occasionally I read some of the steamier passages aloud. Dad cooked nonchalantly throughout, interjecting and laughing periodically. The only troubling moment came when I lifted the box off the table and prepared to carry it upstairs.

Looking alarmed for the first time that day, he said, "I think it's wonderful that you've decided to focus on writing about the broader gay movement and its political history and so forth. That's far better than just doing a personal story."

Perhaps it was the voice of regret. Terror at what he had just done. What he knew I was likely to do with it all. But any ideas I might have had about weaving my memories into a brief history of the gay revolution had been summarily eclipsed by the words, *Last night I made it with a Roman Catholic priest.*

Write about political history? Was he kidding? With *that* kind of material batting its eyelashes at me?

Over the next few months, I pored over the contents of The Box, sometimes so rapt that I would pull up from the middle of a page as though surfacing from an engrossing dream. Certain realizations prompted a reordering of my inner world as pieces of my sometimes puzzling childhood fell into place—*oh,* that's *who that guy was*; or, *so* that's *what Dad was doing there*—and a few memories that had had a hazy quality slid into focus.

The Box was a time capsule, a cardboard safe where, during the two years when he was actively "coming out of the closet," my father stuffed and stored everything that related to his private search for the truth about himself. As I read and transcribed the diaries, articles and letters, I found myself with an ever-deepening understanding of the man behind those words, the complexities and agonies he had lived as he struggled to admit to himself, to his family and to an unsympathetic world that he was gay. If there was value in the material, I realized, it lay in the possibility that reading such a story "from the inside" might help those on the outside to find a similar compassion. For these were not my father's reflections as he is now, a person so comfortable in his life as a gay man that it is difficult to imagine him any other way. These were his words and emotions at the time, when even he had trouble understanding what was happening to him and why.

Although the events (and escapades) recounted in The Box all took place while my parents were still married, at no point during the reading did I feel angry. In fact, it was only after someone asked if it was "infuriating" to read about my father's "infidelity" that I realized it had the potential to be upsetting. But it wasn't, not at all. I was simply fascinated, and curious, and while at times I felt freshly heartbroken for both my parents, it was a beautiful sensation: the kind of heart-opening that leads us to love and understand people more deeply.

It might have been different had The Box disclosed a secret life, an unresolved past, a trail of lies, brutalities or shame. But when my father came out, his secrets were all set free. Through the alchemy of honesty, they had transmuted into truth. And ultimately, truth is a gift of liberation, however painful it might be at the time.

This story would have been incomplete without an honouring of my mother's place in it all, but I chose to treat it with something I knew she would appreciate: brevity. In deference to her private nature, I have kept the details of her life to a minimum. In honour of her musicianship, the structure of her section, Part Three: The Way She Saw It, was inspired by that of a choral requiem.

Names have been changed in most cases for the simple reason that I felt people might appreciate the slight remove, not necessarily from this story but from my take on it. I will never pretend to re-create people as they see themselves and no doubt every person's version of the same events is as different as it is valid. In cases where names were relevant to a larger picture, I have kept them intact. To everyone else, I offer a pseudonymous masque and do hope you all enjoy the ball.

Finally, a few words need to be said on the subject of stereotypes, for they are, in this case as in every other, unfair caricatures of unique individuals, often highly inappropriate and/or inapplicable, and a subtle, maddeningly acceptable form of bigotry.

Gay men do not, of course, all prance, sing show tunes, bake puff pastry or perform mock ballet moves on patios. Of course they do not. It might be fair, however, to say that if one were to walk into a party where men were engaged in the aforementioned activities, one might be *less* inclined to assume those men to be heterosexual. Although they might well be. Just last Christmas, my (male) partner and my brother—both staunch heterosexuals—celebrated their gifts of long underwear by donning them immediately and performing a leaping and twirling version of *The Nutcracker Suite*—"The Nutscratcher Sweets," I believe they called it—for the rest of the family. So anything's possible.

To state the grossly obvious, gay men, like all men, come in every possible shape, size and style; ditto for lesbians and, for that matter, everyone else. Gay men do not talk, move or dance in a particular way, nor do they all share the same tastes or habits. Of course there are millions of examples, but the gay-stereotype-smasher that comes to mind at this instant is the friend of my father's who once devoted several years of his life not to becoming a fashion designer, but to building an airplane—from *scratch*. So let us be clear: an individual is an individual, be they straight, gay, bi, transgender, queer, black, white, dwarf, tall or in all ways absolutely average.

I do not believe in the propagation of stereotypes, although my father may be, at times, a prancing, show-tune-spouting, pastry-baking, ballet-loving example of the stereotypical fairy. (Some people have problems with that word, *fairy*, but I've never felt or used it in anything but the most endearing terms, so have only affectionate associations, as does my father. My apologies to those who equate the word with anything but playful acceptance.)

"I thought gay men were supposed to be tidy," a former boyfriend once remarked upon walking into my father's house, a roving memorial to every paper, book, letter, present, Christmas card, kitchen appliance and rock that has ever come into his possession.

"*Some* gay men are tidy," I replied, a bit peeved by the comment. "But they don't *all* fit the stereotype, you know."

My boyfriend leapt to apologize, the operatic warble of Maria Callas blaring around us. "I don't know why I said that. I can't stand stereotypes," he continued. We put our bags down on the counter next to Nigella Lawson's cookbook *How to Be a Domestic Goddess*. My boyfriend chuckled. "I mean, my dad's probably reading that too."

I swatted him playfully and we looked outside, where my father was hunched over bare-backed in the garden, his T-shirt flung over his head so that the effect was that of a bonnet. My father smiled and stood up when he saw us, his hands flittering around in the air like manic butterflies as he cried, *"Ooooh, helloooo! I've got some bubbly chilling in the fridge!"*

"That's not a stereotype," I said, smiling proudly. "That's my dad."

Throughout the life of this project, I have been newly moved by my father's quest for his most authentic self and for the fullest, most joyful expression of his love.

The story that follows is my attempt at the same.

PART ONE

The Way I Saw It

My childhood was dimly normal: an ordinary red-brick house on an unremarkable street in small-town Ontario. Mother, father, two brothers, a black Labrador named Ida who used to hump the legs of visitors so furiously that she'd leak diarrhea onto the oriental carpet, and a deaf "cleaning lady" (as she was known), who came once a week and ate ketchup sandwiches for lunch. Mrs. Preston had a distended vein that bubbled out from under her eye and loved to sing loud tuneless love songs while dusting with long *pffft*s of Lemon Pledge, so on Tuesdays our house took on an other-planetary feel that I preferred to avoid by going over to Mary Smithey's house to play.

I spent no more time contemplating the concept of home than I thought of ripping up the flooring to see what lay underneath. Home was simply the sound of the front door's creak; the taste of a breeze as it funnelled through my bedroom window and across my cheek; the comforting clang of kitchen pots against classical music and the magic of groceries being transformed into meals; my mother's being there virtually always—*Maaaawm? . . . Yes, in here*; the predictable to-ing and fro-ing of the neighbourhood; the sound of the stones flipping up from the driveway when my father's car pulled in; the fields of tall grasses at the end of the road and their sketch of soft dry gold on my eyes; and the sensation of my teeth as enamelled ice cubes when I played under an evening's snowfall, the crystals falling out of the darkness onto the camber of my tongue.

As most people do, I thought my own family fairly typical. My mother was perfect, except that she ran marathons, was a concert pianist and did not have her ears pierced. Fortunately, none of these quirks was considered strange enough to inspire ridicule from my friends, so they were easily forgiven. As far as I could gather, she was ideal in every other respect. And she eventually even pierced those formerly austere ears, to my great and very vocal delight.

I had grown up believing that my father also floated within the boundaries of normality, he being a professor at the university and, therefore, prone to excusable eccentricities resulting from excessive intelligence or degrees that allegedly proved the equivalent. He took pleasure, for example, in wearing raw silk pyjamas of French design, and while I suspected this was not standard practice for the neighbourhood, I understood that an appreciation for things European was an essential part of being intellectual, so did not mind, as long as he changed into regular clothes before anyone came over to play.

Slightly more distressingly, he also enjoyed skipping down the city sidewalks singing choruses from Gilbert and Sullivan operettas while pumping his elbows out to the sides and snapping his fingers like castanets. I'm sure I loved it as a three-year-old, but by age ten, I had learned to fall out of step and begin idly window-shopping if terse and alarmed pleas for him to stop did not immediately suppress him.

On my seventh birthday, the only one my mother ever missed (she had to visit her sick father in hospital), I had requested hot dogs, coleslaw and chocolate cake iced with Cool Whip. My father, delighted to have been put in charge of my party, listened to my request and then, without consultation, changed the menu to Gruyère soufflé, waxed beans in tarragon butter, and crème brûlée. "It's more *festive*," he explained to my shame-inflamed face, as my friends sat around the table wrinkling their noses and exchanging bulgy-eyed stares. In place of loot bags, each child received a home-copied tape of the Mozart Wind Quintet, and in place of a father, I wished I had a hamster. Or that, at least, is what I shrieked once the last mopey-faced friend had left and I'd burst into tears, running at my father's thighs with my fists. After being sent to my room for being wretched, I filled the stairs with signs saying I HATE SOOFLAY and, in the most powerful protest I could come up with, refused to turn seven.

The day I turned eight, however, I pulled myself up out of the water after a swim in the Trent Canal, arms folded up over my chest, fists rolled under my chin, shivering. I wandered through the Families of Faculties picnic, dripping across a few professors' legs until I reached my father, whose arm was already outstretched. My bum fell into the wedge of his lap as I nestled into him, laying my head against his chest and staring at the dark red nose of his nipple. Above me buzzed numbing talk of political leadership conventions and voting behaviour, as effective a soporific as any I know, and I drooped into a groggy peace. The two things I took note of that afternoon were how the bottom of my thighs felt crazy-glued to the top of his—would I dangle from him when he stood up? I wondered—and how lucky I felt to be entitled to fall asleep on that lap, breathing in the sherry-bread scent of him.

On Sundays, my father liked to bake croissants from scratch, placing the doughy bundles to rise on a ribbed glass hotplate that was as magical to me as a witch's cauldron. When the little crescents had puffed up dutifully, my father would lift the damp dishtowel and call us over to witness the miracle known as "doubling" before transferring the croissants to the hot stove and clicking on the oven light. There we would sit, my brothers and I, forever pushing each other out of the way—you're hogging the whole window, move ó-ver—watching the anemic goop transform into crisp, gorgeous pastry. Never did we manage to wait the suggested ten minutes before plucking—ow!—a fresh wrap of buttery gold and juggling it onto a plate. While my father put on choral music and began conducting dreamily to an invisible choir, my brothers and I would snap off the pastry's pointed end and watch the steam coil out like a genie. The next task was to extract the stretchy white interior and fill the hollow with globs of rapidly melting butter and raspberry jam. As the Verdi Requiem blared chromatic drama across the kitchen, my father would sit with his eyes closed, alternately biting into his croissant and directing the music with a poised conductor's hand, groaning with a combination of culinary and musical pleasure. With crumbles of greasy, golden flakes collecting on our lips and fingers, and the kitchen assuming the auditory grandeur of a cathedral, it was easy to love my father and his peculiarities.

• • •

When my brother Paul turned ten (and I was still frustratingly, single-digitly, eight), Dad dispensed with baking for several months, pronouncing that it was time for Paul and me to begin attending church. After the initial ooh-aah over the stained glass windows, the long shiny benches, and the unreachable-by-spitball ceilings, Paul and I dripped with boredom. The porridge-faced minister preached monotonously and could no more carry a tune than turn a cartwheel. Each time the congregation sang, Paul and I would cover our ears, proclaiming that their intonation was so bad it hurt our teeth.

After a few Sundays of this, the only way my father could entice us to attend church was by promising us something so implausible as to be miraculous: a post-benedictory trip to McDonald's. The bribe worked spectacularly well, in that we agreed to go to the service, but as everyone else sang tired hymns (from books with pages that I was convinced, for some reason, were made from Jesus's dried skin), my brother and I would whisper-sing the Big Mac jingle we'd turned into a psalm:

> *Two all-beef pa-a-a-a-tties,*
> *spe-e-e-e-cial sauce, lettuce, che-e-e-e-se,*
> *pickles, onions on a sesame, a sesame,*
> *thou sayeth now a se-e-e-same,*
> *may I beseech thee a sesame,*
> *a sesame seed bu-u-u-u-n.*
> *A-a-a-a-men.*

On Communion days, we would accompany my father to the altar and kneel beside him while he received of the wafer and wine. Because we were too young to partake, the minister would lay his hand on our heads and wish us eternal life. The first time this happened after the bribe had kicked in, the blessing went thus:

"May you have eternal life, child."

Paul: "Actually, I'm having a cheeseburger."

My father separated his hands from prayer position and gave Paul's bottom a light swat.

Shortly thereafter, my father abandoned the fast-food sacrament and returned to long Sunday mornings at home with the croissant ritual. We were all the happier, the healthier and, I dare say, the more blessed for it.

I do not remember my mother being part of the croissant extravaganzas. As I recall, she would have toast and go out for a run. Or shopping. Or upstairs. Or wherever it was she went when I lost track of her, which was as infrequently as I could manage it. My father flitted in and out of the nest of our lives like most men of his time, but I thought of my mother as the spiral of sticks itself, her limbs the very twigs that held our home together.

It never occurred to me that she might have been less than fulfilled in her role as Circle of Twigs, that there might have been things she wanted to do in her life besides shop for groceries, make spaghetti, load the dishwasher and do our laundry. She was every bit as dynamic as my father, as fun and as funny, as interesting and interested in the world, but her personal passions waned just as my father's might have done had he been forced to leave the stimulating environment of the university and find joy instead in the six interchangeable parts of the vacuum cleaner.

My mother was not a domestic creature by nature. Keeping house did not, as it were, light her fire. When Mrs. Preston came to clean for the first time, she was considerate enough to assure my mother that she would never tell anyone how messy our house was. Which it was not, really, but nor was it, say, the picture of sparkle and organization.

"It would be easier for your mother if she weren't so bright" was a neighbour's offhanded comment one day as she sat in our kitchen waiting for my mother. Mrs. Bludge had come over to ask about piano lessons for her son, but my mother was in the middle of practising. Mrs. Bludge said she would wait because she didn't want to interrupt my mother's music.

"Oh, it's not my mother's music," I replied. "It's Schumann."

Mrs. Bludge looked puzzled, so I added: "And she's still not at the really tricky bit, so it's still going to go on for a long time."

Which is when Mrs. Bludge looked around the room and made the *it would be easier for your mother* comment, intended as either an insult or a compliment, I wasn't quite sure. But as I stood there looking around at our chaotic kitchen—the jumble of dishes on the counter looked like a page from the Schumann concerto—I can say only that it didn't *feel* very complimentary.

It is true that my mother was bored in her role as stay-at-home wife and mother, but she bore up so admirably under the boredom that none of us really noticed. Cheerful she was almost always, though not in the hyper-expressive way of the truly depressed mothers in the neighbourhood. There was tremendous splash in her when she was inspired (by music, great books, lively dinner debates), but she was mostly calm, tranquil water. A lake we lived by and took for granted, daily.

I was vaguely aware that my mother did not spring to life in the kitchen, a suspicion that was confirmed the year she unwrapped the *I Hate to Cook Cookbook*, a Christmas gift to herself. She was not a baker, as I was—happily reigning over my Easy-Bake Oven dominion with a dedication and panache my mother did not seem to possess.

For me, the feeling I had while baking approached bliss,

the process of tearing open those sturdy packages of cake mix and pouring them—*splosh!*—into the bowl. The water would be measured with a scientist's precision, the measuring cup teetering in my hands as I carried it from the sink to the bowl carefully, tongue out to one side, so as not to drip. My small hill of cake mix would transform into sensuous batter, and with a spatula the size of a toothbrush I would scrape the sweet goop into two miniature aluminum cake pans and ease them into my toy oven.

Apparently, my mother used to love watching me stare through the little oven window at my cakes browning under the heating mechanism: a hot bare lightbulb. It wasn't so much the look on my face, she said, as the way I sat, my body and neck bent at just the right angle to allow me to see inside without getting my face burned, the way I was so mesmer-ized by the simple miracle contained within that warm little tin box. Between the croissants and my saucer-sized cakes, baking was my earliest devotion.

I do not know why having an oven ten times the size altered the experience so profoundly, but it seems that it did, for despite repeated efforts, my mother was never able to muster the same Easy-Bake Ecstasy. More than once, she pulled black-burnt loaf pans out of the oven, huffing as she heaved them onto the stovetop.

"Weren't you watching?" I once asked timidly.

"No," she mumbled in frustration. "I was working on a new Chopin étude."

• • •

After Mrs. Preston and her Lemon Pledge joined the family picture, my mother would remain at the piano for longer stretches, learning the formidable Rachmaninoff Second Piano Concerto, among others, while my brothers and I watched episodes of *The Partridge Family* on television. Occasionally, she performed as a soloist with the local symphony orchestra, but she was leagues above them and everyone knew it, though in good Anglo-Saxon fashion everyone smiled and said nothing of the sort. Eventually, my mother put Rachmaninoff on a back burner and took up running, replacing her nondescript leather shoes with swooshy trainers and making ever-widening circles around the house. Next thing we knew, she'd gone off to Ottawa to run a marathon. The news had no effect on me whatsoever, apart from formulating in my mind an understanding of big cities as places where people run around and around to the point of exhaustion for reasons baffling to everyone but them.

Another of my mother's notable characteristics was her affinity for birds, and animals in general. I could not possibly count the number of birds that were tended in shoeboxes over the years, creatures that had either bashed themselves into windows, dropped prematurely out of nests or been the brief playthings of neighbourhood cats. For each one she would make a nest of Kleenex, feed them with eyedroppers, a heating pad and Bach. Most of them died. And she greeted every small death with a wince of such pain that my brothers and I would leave the room.

Broken wings she would always leave to the vet, ferrying the birds (and once a hawk, which nearly tore her to shreds as she gathered it up) over to his clinic on the rural route behind our house. Years later, the same vet told me my mother was one of the most incredible people he'd ever met. "Why," I laughed, "because of all the birds?" "No," he said. "Because of everything."

As a young woman, my mother completed her undergraduate degree in music at the University of Western Ontario and, upon graduation, was awarded a bursary to further her piano studies in Paris. From there, she won a Canada Council scholarship to study at the Royal Academy of Music in London, England, where she took lessons with a number of master pianists, including the renowned Myra Hess. The first time my mother told me about this illustrious period of her life, I watched a smile of serenity blossom across her face and ached to learn more. Every day she would walk more than an hour to the Royal Academy of Music, she recounted to me, enraptured audience of one. The words *Royal Academy* suggested such romance and elegance that I clapped my hands together and held them under my chin. There, she continued, she would close herself into one of the rehearsal rooms and spend the entire day, eight to ten hours, playing the piano, pausing only to eat the sandwich she had brought with her.

(Practising eight hours and eating a sandwich? Uh, was that the good part?)

Furthering the glamour of the story, my mother told me she rented a room at the back of a house in an unfortunate part of London, sharing the place with the Gutters, a family of five.

On Fridays, Mrs. Gutter would pull a metal washtub into the kitchen, heat a large pot of water on the stove and pour it into the tub. Because my mother was the guest, she was the first one to use the water, a privilege for which she was extremely grateful. She said she often wondered how that sixth person bathing in the same water felt. Thriftiness in accommodations freed up the rest of her savings for the purchase of a grand piano, and while it just barely fit into her room, she was able to tuck her bed under the instrument's black breadth and sleep beneath the soundboard.

"Where did you keep your clothes?" I asked, still on the lookout for the story's charm.

Her answer: "I don't remember. I must not have had any."

My mother and father dated, on and off, over a period of seven years before getting married. They had met as students at the University of Western Ontario when my mother was in her first year and my father in his last. The first time he saw my mother sitting on the stairs of the university's music building (where they were both studying), my father remembers, "I just wanted to put my arms around her and cuddle her."

My father graduated with a degree in Economics and Political Science and a certificate in musical education, and went on to the University of Toronto to do an MA. He had wanted to give my mother his fraternity pin (a sort of pre-engagement), but she discussed it with her father and declined with the explanation that she didn't really know what she wanted to do with her future—and that seemed reasonable to my father.

The following year, they both found themselves living abroad—my mother in France, my father in England—and their connection continued through correspondence, visits and the odd shared adventure. At one point, my mother broke off the relationship and my father remembers being devastated. The two went their separate ways and my father threw himself into writing his Doctorate of Philosophy at Oxford. (Apparently, he hoped to turn his dissertation into "something of a Sibelius symphony," but as the subject matter was Elections and Politics in Canada West under Responsible Government, 1847–1863, it was difficult to meld the two ideas.)

After a separation of nearly two years, the angels of fate (and the careful strategizing of a common friend) ensured that my mother and father were seated beside each other at a concert in London. They chatted enthusiastically during the party afterwards and my father remembers driving off at the end of the night "floating on a cloud." They spent the next few months having picnics and attending concerts, though never on Friday nights lest my mother miss her coveted bath.

After my father completed his symphonic parliamentary thesis and returned to Canada, my mother moved to Vienna to continue her piano studies and Spartan sandwich routine. Apparently, Vienna (or the Viennese—I can't remember) drove her a bit mad and she never really warmed to the place. But the deciding moment came when my mother received a pearl necklace in the mail from my father. Then and there she decided to ship her piano from England to Canada, and she and my father were married later that year.

That's my father's version, at any rate. My mother doesn't remember receiving a gift of any kind. "Your dad and I split up for a while and sometime after that we saw each other back in England and things kind of picked up again. But there was no necklace. I don't remember him giving me anything. I came back from Europe because my money ran out. And then we got married. You know . . . people were expected to do that in those days."

It seems odd to write about my parents as a couple, for even my early memories of them are as separate entities. Their bedroom contained twin beds, something I thought nothing of, assuming Mary Smithey's parents shared a bed only because they must have been too poor to buy two. My mother and father always got along pleasantly, but I do not have a memory of them actually touching. In an innocent and unalarmed way, I always assumed that they lived together for the simple reason that they both happened to be related to my brothers and me.

Their love was music, in that it was the sacred hearth of their lives. Though as a child I never put it in such terms, I believe I saw them as both being wedded to music and, through that, to each other. (Once, my father mentioned that one of the things that had drawn him to my mother was that she had been more interested in music than necking. When I queried her on the subject, her response was "Ditto.") They were both accomplished pianists and sometimes played duets or music-for-four-hands piano. Most of their friends were musicians of one kind or another, and typical social get-togethers involved my father conducting people in the choral rounds of a spoof composer known as P.D.Q. Bach, while my mother accompanied them on the piano. There were great eruptions of laughter as people muffed a line or got lost, and although my brothers and I would feign annoyance—*we're trying to sleep!*—we secretly loved it.

When people came over to our house, they always brought their French horn. Or their bassoon—a word I learned before the word *gun*—or their double bass or clarinet or the latest recording of so-and-so playing such-and-such. Many a night we kids would lie in bed listening to the sounds of my parents and their friends playing chamber music, and I would lift into a transcendence I have never tried to name.

Music was my mother tongue; it was the language of home.

Three international events of 1969 made it a pivotal year for my family: the Stonewall Riots in New York City; the Criminal Law Amendment Act in Canada; and our family holiday in the south of France, where, to my mother's great relief, I was toilet-trained.

The first event was so distant and irrelevant to our family that it went unnoticed at the time. The Stonewall Inn was a popular gay bar in Manhattan's West Village. While police raids on such establishments were not uncommon, by 1969, lesbians, gays, bisexuals, transsexuals and queers (now known as the LGBTQ community) were fed up with the routine harassment. Every intolerable situation has its boiling point and this one was reached on June 28, when instead of submitting to police arrest, the employees and patrons of the Stonewall Inn resisted and fought back. There followed the massive demonstrations and riots now known to history as "Stonewall," the watershed incident that led to vocal, widespread and organized demands for LGBTQ rights, and the moment, it is said, that the gay revolution was born.

Who knew that raid/riot/demand-for-rights would have any effect on our young Canadian family? But it would, in an indirect way. Although not for another decade.

Closer to home, the second momentous event of 1969 involved a hip, progressive Canadian politician by the name of Pierre Elliott Trudeau, whose landmark Criminal Law Amendment Act decriminalized, among other things, abortion, contraception and homosexuality between consenting adults. "There's no place for the state in the bedrooms of the nation," Trudeau famously told reporters. "What's done in private between adults doesn't concern the Criminal Code."

My father would have been paying close attention to those words, not because he felt they had any personal relevance—they didn't; not then—but because he was a devoted Liberal and a recently tenured professor of political studies. And, like millions of other Canadians, he was a supporter of the "just society" and a big fan of Pierre Trudeau.

To those two grand events of 1969, I contributed a third, namely the planting of my sweet petunia onto a white plastic potty and the happy sound of urine sprinkling down. The rite of passage took place in the village of Bardigues, where my family was spending the summer, and the setting made such an impression that for many years I continued to free-associate France with urine.

In 1970, my mother gave birth to a third child and less than a year later, in an act of intrepid insanity, my parents decided to take all three of us on another European escapade. Stoically, we trundled across Madeira, the Canary Islands, Spain and France, dragging, as my mother recalls, bags of dirty diapers (not mine!) through endless museums, cathedrals and laby-rinthine cobblestone streets. My parents lost only one of us, somewhere in rural Spain.

Our train from Granada to Madrid had stopped in a small Andalusian station. My father, I am told, headed off the train in search of something for us all to eat and a few seconds later, my older brother, Paul, asked if he could go with him. *Sure sure*, said my mother with characteristic insouciance, propping up my sleeping head with one hand and my baby brother with the other. Five-year-old Paul puffed out his chest proudly, heaved open the compartment door and went slapping down the train corridor into the world of adults.

After a time, the train's whistle blew, my mother glanced briefly out the window and we hissed forward. The small town's few houses disappeared and were quickly replaced by goats on hilltops doing their horizontal chew. As the train careered along, my father appeared in the aisle juggling bread, cheese, fruit and a bottle of wine. It was then, seeing Dad without child in tow, that my mother panicked and told him that Paul had followed him off the train. Who knows how they managed it (my father possesses a useful talent for the hysterical), but as I recall, my parents got that train to whinny itself to a halt and wobble backwards through the rough Spanish countryside until we pulled into the station in reverse, only to find Paul, blond and bony-kneed, standing alone on the platform. He was stolid until he saw our faces. Then, a thousand tears shot from his body all at once.

My parents expressed such gratitude to the train conductor that, following a path of childhood logic, I entertained fantasies of having once been part of a much larger family with various siblings who had been forgotten at train stations all over Europe, the other conductors not having been so kind as to go back and pick them up.

• • •

Eventually, I came to accept that two brothers were all I had ever had. In my early years, they were both my dearest life companions and creatures as strange to me as the plantar warts on my left foot: fascinating to pick at, those strange tentacles that had embedded themselves deep into my being, but mysterious in their purpose, other than as a vague annoyance, something crudely intriguing. I could not have imagined that I would grow up to adore my brothers; when I was young, that notion would have been as inconceivable to me as falling in love with my warts.

From the time he was able to admire them, Paul was fascinated by the productions of his own body, famously spreading the contents of his diaper the full circumference of his crib and head, while my mother hosted her first University Women's Club tea downstairs. The last time he and I ever took a bath together was the night he invented a game called Lumberyard, in which he stood up, bent over and produced three brown logs, encouraging me to catch them as they came out of the mill. Instead of growing out of the "bowel narcissism," as my mother came to term it, his captivation only grew in sophistication over the years, and when we get together for visits we are still, to the present day, treated to commentary on his morning eliminations.

Paul could be terrific fun, even in non-anally-fixated ways. He was (and remains) a great creator of games and a natural leader, once inspiring hordes of neighbourhood children to host our own version of the summer Olympics complete with elaborate opening ceremonies (I can't remember which of us was chosen to run around the block holding the flashlight aloft like a torch), and hyper-precise timing, scorekeeping and statistics. Most of the time, however, Paul was an intimidating mystery to me, prone as he was at age ten to willingly spend an afternoon reading a biography of Winston Churchill and then positing theories on war strategies and little-known undercurrents in British society of the time. In truth, I found it easier to relate to his bowels.

I'm sure my younger brother was born with a proper name, but from the moment we began calling him Flip (for no particular reason), we never used his given name again. Flip could only get to sleep by lying down and bobbling his head rhythmically against the pillow, something that looked demented but was apparently normal. His best friend, Little Boy Cowboy, shot him in the stomach one day in a back field—there was, indeed, a small scar—and had a sister named Beaushamblah. We never met either of them, but Flip spent many a day making Lego sandwiches for them in the backyard.

At three, he refused to eat anything but "hat bacon" (a piece of bologna fried until it puffed up into a hat shape), peanut butter sandwiches (butter on the waymost bottom, then honey, then peanut butter on the waymost top, crusts off, sliced diagonally), bananas, strawberry yogourt, a pastry my father used to make called "cheese puffs," and green beans. The diet (slightly modified a few years later: pancakes in place of hat bacon) nourished him to the age of nineteen, the year he finally agreed to wear shorts. To protest a much-despised teacher (who taught him to read, horrid thing), Flip walked backwards to school for the entire first term of grade two.

Years later the neighbours confided to us how much they had enjoyed the daily reverse parade. "Yes, he's quite idiosyncratic," my father replied. To which I clapped my hand to my mouth and *tee-hee-hee*'d up the stairs. I assumed that "idiosyncratic" was a grown-up, professorial way of saying "idiotic."

Paul, Flip and I had our sibling laughs, and plenty of them, our games and silly voices, but we also fought, fiercely and dramatically, over all the standard things—cheating at a game, being "gross" or generally annoying, hogging the bathroom—inevitably proclaiming our revulsion for one another with loud and careless pride. The sibling battles upset my father terribly, but he was the furthest thing from helpful when it came to resolving spats, a fact made clear by his default response (spoken with hands flapping around helplessly): "Kids, kids! Now, now, now . . . stop trying to get each other's goats!"

My father was not a natural disciplinarian. (*Why have discipline when you can have fun?* I imagine him saying.) The task of imparting discipline fell to my mother; although, being a lover of fun herself, she was reluctant to play the heavy and was often frustrated by having to assume the role. While my father busied himself or just looked the other way, it was she who laid down the law (when necessary), she who had us cleaning up the milk we spilled, she who enforced bedtimes, et cetera.

There was never any question as to who wore the pants in the family, but never did that prompt us to wonder if that meant my dad wore the skirt. So to speak. I knew lots of kids with strong-willed mothers and namby-pamby dads. Nothing out of the ordinary there.

Something a bit less common was that my mother sometimes wore my brother's clothing. I don't remember when it started, only that one day I noticed that the green jeans I used to see on Paul's body were now on hers. As well as his sweatshirt. He was probably about fifteen and rapidly outgrowing "perfectly good clothes," as my mother called them. So, being what's known as "petite," she began to wear them.

Or, being what's known as "tomboyish," she began to wear them.

Actually, she wasn't a tomboy; she was just beautiful in a natural, short-haired, no-makeup, independent, athletic and intelligent sort of way. My mother never used the term *feminist*, but that is what she was. And while she may not have put it in exactly these words, she felt that fashion was for airheads and shopping was a tedious waste of time. So she wore my brother's hand-me-downs—or hand-me-ups, I guess they would be—and got on with her day.

If my father had had his way, my name today would be Amaryllis, and while I am grateful to my mother for the many things she has done for me over my lifetime, her opposition to that floral moniker rates among the primary ones. My father's second choice of given name was Filomena, as there is a lovely sixteenth-century madrigal about a girl named Filomena and wouldn't it be wonderful to have a child so named, but my mother categorically nixed that one too. Bless her heart.

I almost died at birth, six weeks early and tiny as a crab. The doctors wrung me out and pumped me up with new blood, which somehow helped, though it required them to shave my head so drastically that I waddled through my first years of life bald as a potato.

When my hair did grow in, it did so with an eye for re-prisal, its fists raised in wiry curls that made the more racist elders in the family worry about my origins. These were not luscious curls; they were thick knuckly masses, something a (brief) boyfriend was once generous enough to inform me was the stuff that makes up a rhinoceros's horn. As a child, I moaned about my not-at-all-silky hair, brushed the mass a hundred times a night (an exercise that only exploded the situation, like yeast given sugar) and, at my mother's insistence, kept it as short as possible.

Early childhood drawings have me illustrating myself thus: two arms, two legs, a happy face surrounded by a full 360 degrees of curly hair. Just one great squiggly line going round and round across the top of the head, all the way down under the chin and up the other side. (Note: thirty years later, my son's drawings depicted his mother identically.)

Throughout elementary school, I strove to model myself on Laura Ingalls from *Little House on the Prairie*: a brave and good soul with silken braids. I failed miserably, my thick, wiry hair giving me more of a Pippi Longstocking look (think horizontal braids). After being laughed out of the playground for arriving in a bonnet, I took to sleeping with a frilly white nightcap and reciting prayers on my knees like my blessed heroine. I would fall asleep feeling pious and satisfied, but was a thrasher of a sleeper, inevitably flinging the ruffled cap to the ground sometime during the night. In the morning, I would roll my wildly curly self out of bed and retrieve the cap from the floor ashamedly, even on occasion muttering under my breath, "Sorry, God."

I do not recall at what age I convinced my mother to let me have my hair straightened, only that I must have been quite small. The hairdresser simply blew it dry, strand by strand, with healthy applications of hairspray, until I looked as though I had cozied up to a steamroller.

All the way home, I stroked my Saran Wrap hair. Dreamily, I rolled down the car window to feel it blow in straight lines across my face. I was elated and begged my mother to learn the technique herself, "Please, please buy hairspray!"—she smiled flatly; she never bought cosmetics of any kind—they were for stupid people, she told me rather bluntly. "But I want to keep it this way forever!" I pleaded, running a hand over my straw-straight hair.

When we got home, I wandered to the end of the driveway so that the world could see me. I flipped my head from side to side, relishing the *straightness*, waiting for someone to walk by and comment, but no one did and eventually I sat down in the gravel. Briefly, I recalled bleaker times from my old life when my brothers had sneaked pebbles into my hair, me oblivious to the joke until I laid my head down on the pillow at night and felt the bumps.

No longer.

For the first time, I could draw my fingers from the top of my skull all the way down the length of my hair to the ends. It was heavenly. I did it over and over, decided I would stay up all night doing it, and then got the inspired idea of putting a small stone at the crown of my head to feel it slide, unimpeded, down the smooth strands. *N-n-n-n-plonk*. It was so delicious I did it again. Then with sand, which tickled the curve of my scalp as it slid down the slick slope. Like ice. For the rest of the afternoon, my head was the hill for handful after handful of pebble skiers. I believe I charged them admission when they rode the finger-lift up my arm.

No surprises as to how the fantasy ended, which was with my mom's exclamation, "What on earth did you do to your hair, we'll have to wash it!" *Trrrrrrrring!*

Curls again.

From that day on, I assumed them as my life's curse.

That and school, whose purpose never came clear to me during all of the eighteen years that I attended. In kindergarten it was discovered that I could read, so while the other children played, I was sent out into the hallway to do spelling flashcards with an "advanced" grade eight student who found the exercise so dull that no doubt she wished she had been labelled "retarded" instead. I greeted each day with a leaden dread, my stomach a tangle of glass-tipped threads that once pierced my bladder and released a morning's worth of urine during storytime. The sensation was one of blessed relief, like the exhalation after holding one's breath, a warm wash against the backs of my thighs that was comforting only until we all stood up and a dark circle revealed itself where I had been sitting. Naturally, I found reason to busy myself with something on the other side of the room, listening to the teacher's stern pronouncement—that someone had been very, *very* bad—and donning a look of surprise and disapproval comparable to those of my classmates. For the rest of the morning, my white tights sagged with the cold memory of that release, burning and scratching my legs as I walked, and freezing like a patch of yellow snow on my bum when we were let outside for recess.

When my mother complained about the flashcard drudgery—peeing one's pants is a sign of stress, I heard her confide to a neighbour—she was invited to a meeting with my teacher and the principal, both of whom thought it would be better if I were taken out of the class and moved into grade one. My mother said she preferred that I stay where I was, as all I really wanted or needed to do was play with my friends, but the teacher insisted that I be put among children of the same ability. "Otherwise," she concluded with a rhetorical question that spun my mother's eyeballs, "how is she ever going to learn how to conform?"

In the end, my mother won, but the truth is that my teacher was right. For in a few months I will turn forty-five and still I have not the slightest idea how to conform.

"Close your eyes—and try not to *feel*." These were the instructions I gave to my father as he lay back in the reclining chair of the family room and prepared to count to ten, and I scampered off to find a hiding place. I was probably four or five years old. My plan—I could not imagine why I hadn't thought of it before—was to hide behind his back. He would never think to look there. The only technical difficulty I envisioned was that I would have to crawl *under* his reclined body. Thus the instructions.

Always the good sport, my father did as he was told. I burrowed into a spot beneath his shoulder blade, and when he reached "TEN!" he bounded up and wandered around the house looking for me in all the usual places, accenting his search with many a declaration about how challenging it was to find me.

Scarcely containing my laughter, I sat on the reclining chair, nestling into the warm imprint his body had left on the leather. As I heard his footsteps approaching, my entire body tensed with excitement, so full of glee that I had to stuff my hands between my legs to keep all the giggles inside. He clapped his hands and shrieked when he saw me.

"How did you get there?"

My laughter slapped every wall in the room. "I was hiding *underneath* you!"

That was the first time I realized how clever I was.

The second occasion came near the end of a long drive

to a cottage, where we were to spend a month of our summer holidays when I was four. It was late, and the gravel rumbled beneath our tires as our car wound along a maze of narrow, dark roads. Not a street or house light in sight. Black sculptures of trees on either side.

My parents were muttering in the front seat, consulting handwritten directions under the thin beam of the car's interior light and pushing frustration and question marks back and forth at each other across a small map. Then, a solemn declaration sounded from the back seat.

"I know where we are," Paul announced gloomily. "We're *lost*."

"No we're not," I insisted, pointing towards the front of the car. "Look, Daddy has his headlights on!"

For a few happy moments, my parents' voices lifted into laughter, the mood in the car lightening so palpably that I was convinced I had struck brilliance again. "We can't be lost if we can see where we're going, silly Paul!"

Eventually we arrived at the cottage, as I had known we would, and had a beautiful holiday full of creaky screen doors, weedy swimming, my dad reading *Gourmet* magazine while tanning himself on the dock, and evenings that sparkled with loon calls. Some mornings I awoke before dawn, pushed my arms into the sleeves of a pale yellow sweater my grandmother had knitted me, and sat with my cat on a steep granite cliff overlooking the lake. Chin on my knees. The cardigan's top button a hard candy between my teeth. And the day's first light like soft warm ribbons in my hair.

Mine was a carefree childhood. When I went missing, someone looked for me; when we got lost, we found our way. We laughed, played, ate well, loved each other.

All the essentials.

BATHTUBS AND POLITICAL EDUCATION

One way to encourage two children out of the bathtub: *Okay, kids, it's time to get out of the bathtub.*

Another way: *Okay, kids, I have a tube of toothpaste behind my back. Whoever chooses the hand with the toothpaste in it gets to stay in a little longer.*

A third way, and the option preferred by professors of political science who are keen to see their children grow up with a modicum of vital political knowledge: "Okay, kids, I'm going to teach you the names of all the prime ministers of Canada. Whichever one of you can recite them back to me the fastest gets to stay in the bath the longest."

When one is born the child of a professor of political science, one assumes as normal the following: spending the chilly evenings of several weeks going door-to-door—not unlike Jehovah's Witnesses, come to think of it—canvassing for the Liberal candidate of your riding; being allowed to stay up late *only* on the nights of leadership conventions and having to feign enthusiasm when what's-his-name wins; living with a large poster of Prime Minister Trudeau's silhouette in the garage and his annual family-portrait Christmas card hanging prominently in the front hall, all year long; and being asked to learn the names of prime ministers as part of a bedtime ritual.

Thus, a typical scene from the Wearing household *circa* 1972: A corduroy-clad man with black horn-rimmed glasses and short, curly hair climbs the stairs, adjusts his glasses as he notices himself in the hallway mirror, walks four steps down the hallway and opens the bathroom door. His two eldest children, aged five and six, instantly drop their bath toys and shout in unison: *"MacdonaldMackenzieMacdonaldAbbottThompsonBowellTupper LaurierBordenMeighenKingMeighenKingBennettKingSt.Laurent DiefenbakerPearsonTrudeau!"*

To be accurate, it wasn't quite in unison. While the litany was recited perfectly by Paul without so much as a fumble, I, being more of a musical learner by nature and therefore inclined to focus on the lyricism of words rather than the accuracy, rattled off something along the lines of *"McDonald'sCandy McDonald's . . . Tom'sson'sBowels . . . Uproar . . . B-b-boredMeKing KingMeKingBenNetKingSayLeron . . . D-EasyBakeOvenTrudeau!"*

Paul always won.

Until one night I burst into tears in the middle of my stumbling recitation and my father suggested we return to the earlier ritual of choosing the hand that held the toothpaste. At this, I was impressively adept.

Once we were prime-ministered, brushed and into our pyjamas, my father would read to us, not from *Winnie-the-Pooh*, as most of my other five-year-old friends' parents were doing at the time, but *Great Expectations*. Being a Dickens fan, my father felt it important that we be exposed at a young age. I do not remember much of the story itself, although the mere mention of the title brings up a vivid image of young Pip helping the convict file the shackle from his leg, as well as a memory of being very glad I didn't live in England, where such things went on.

I'm not sure how much of the story Paul and I understood, but I do remember that my father encouraged us to ask him to explain unfamiliar words, and we certainly had plenty to choose from.

From that room, too, the daylight was completely excluded, and it had an airless smell that was oppressive. A fire had been lately kindled in the damp old-fashioned grate, and it was more disposed to go out than to burn up, and the reluctant smoke which hung in the room seemed colder than the clearer air—like our own marsh mist. Certain wintry branches of candles on the high chimneypiece faintly lighted the chamber; or it would be more expressive to say, faintly troubled its darkness. It was spacious, and I dare say had once been handsome, but every discernible thing in it was covered with dust and mold, and dropping to pieces.

Generally Paul and I would choose only one or two words per paragraph to ask about; otherwise, the story never seemed to get going.

"What's *dis-earn-a-bull*?"

My father would stop, look pensive. "Something that's perceptible. You can see it or perhaps sense it. *There is a discernible smell coming from Paul's side of the bed just now*, for example."

For me, the memorable thing about *Great Expectations* was not so much the story as the cello song of my father's voice, the way we lay on the bed all together, limbs relaxed against limbs. Often I would drift from the storyline and simply enjoy my father's pleasure, the animated way that he read, the way different voices felt when I closed my eyes, the funny way the English had of saying *ought* or *I know not what*, and how much my father seemed to love Dickens's wit, laughing out loud when something amused him. We did not learn typical stories from my father; what we learned was the joy that can be found in the telling. Such an invaluable lesson.

How it has fed me throughout my life.

My early musical career was a sweet scene, beginning as it did on the "cello" at age four. Born tiny as a crab, I was only slightly larger than a lobster by this point, and I found it too difficult to hold and manoeuvre even a child's-size cello. I was therefore given a viola (an instrument moderately larger and lower in pitch than its cousin the violin) to turn upside down and hold between my thighs as a makeshift cello. This was, I was later told, awfully cute.

Because I still existed in that glorious but oh-so-brief phase of childhood graced by unselfconsciousness, I thought nothing of holding a little viola between my legs and sawing off one brutalized note after the next. I even attended several rehearsals of the Peterborough Youth Orchestra, sitting at the end of the cello section, eight-year-olds towering around me, my mother at my side. I joined them for only one or two pieces, both requiring little more than a couple long bowed notes and a few shorter ones, and was invited to play in their upcoming concert.

The day of the first Youth Orchestra concert is a shard of a memory, pointy and uncomfortable to hold. My dress was tight around my neck, my tights itchy and pulling at the crotch. There was a lot of yowling and straining of string instruments being massacred by children with hopeful parents in the audience, mine among them. When it was my turn to join the orchestra, I remember not wanting to play and being gently coaxed to sit down. The guillotine dropped when I set my very wee instrument between my legs and heard the snickering, looked out at the small audience and noticed people watching me, some of them pointing, many of them laughing quietly behind their hands. The phrase *awfully cute* sounded above the rest of the whispers, but I heard it as "awful, cute" and the rest is a hot-faced blur. I don't believe I played a note.

So much for the "cello."

I did take up the full-sized instrument later, at the roaring age of seven, alongside my father, who decided it would be fun to learn together. I don't know how long it lasted—a year at most—but I remember it as a laboured period punctuated by fatherly frustration, a lot of sighing and *no-no-no*s and *try-it-again*s.

One might assume that two pianistic parents would produce three little Mozartesque offspring with the same ease and inevitability that two Mexican parents produce a Spanish-speaking brood, but that was not the case in our family. We all had music spun into our cell tissue, but we sloughed off any attempts at lessons and teaching as soon as we were old enough to protest. My parents didn't insist; neither was the pushy type, fortunately for us. My mother spent her days giving piano lessons to children, so probably did not have much inspiration left at the end of the day to wrestle her children through more of the same. And my father was busy making other music.

I knew that my father was a professor of political studies at Trent University, but what he actually did was a mystery of books, papers and unbearably boring discussions about elections,

Pierre Trudeau and the Liberal Party. In the evenings, however, he would often return to the university to do things that were exciting and made sense, like conducting chamber choirs or Gilbert and Sullivan operettas. Though he didn't lead a choir or direct an operetta every week, his heading back to Trent in the evenings for rehearsals was a fairly common occurrence.

No doubt my mother resented him for dedicating himself all day to intellectual pursuits, coming home to eat, then dashing out to dedicate himself to musical pursuits—although I detected no such resentment at the time. Her own intellectual and musical aspirations were so routinely and consummately consumed by the demands of domesticity that none of us noticed it when that happened, and no doubt it did, daily.

So while my mother stayed home washing dirty dishes, playing bingo with Flip, and wishing, perhaps, that she could have been channelling Chopin at the piano, she shipped Paul and me off to rehearsals with my father, and we were happy to oblige. Or rather, my dad adored taking Paul and me to rehearsals with him and we were happy to oblige. Not sure which. Either way, we loved going.

Trent University at night was this: long, empty hallways, silence, and air that smelled like sand. Endless hiding places. Tall, heavy doors that opened onto rooms that went *hush*. Wide carpeted expanses where we could run wild, diving into imaginary pools until we came away with rugburns on our elbows.

Once we'd exhausted ourselves with exploring, Paul and I would heave open the door of the university's Wenjack Theatre and hear music rising up from the stage. We would wander through the amphitheatre's row upon row of cushy seating, running our fingers along the fabric until we found just the right spot to settle in and watch our father bob around the stage inspiring people to sing silly songs about silly things. Pretending to fall in love. Pretending to be rejected. Pretending to be gondoliers. Pretending to be Japanese. And all of them daft, no matter who they were pretending to be, because that is the nature of Gilbert and Sullivan operettas.

It was better than television.

On the way home, my father would sing an assortment of ridiculous libretti that made the drive go by like a finger-snap:

I am the very model of a modern Major-General
I've information vegetable, animal, and mineral
I know the kings of England, and I quote the fights historical
From Marathon to Waterloo, in order categorical.

I'm very well acquainted, too, with matters mathematical.
I understand equations, both the simple and quadratical.
About binomial theorem I'm teeming with a lot o' news
With many cheerful facts about the square of the hypotenuse.

On cue, Paul and I would rise up in the back seat (pre-seat-belt era), Paul conducting with the same verve and enthusiasm my father had displayed earlier in the evening, and the two of us chiming back the chorus:

With many cheerful facts about the square of the hypotenuse!

By the time the performance dates arrived, Paul and I had attended so many rehearsals, we knew everyone's lines, spoken or sung. We loved the thrill of the performances, the costumes and excitement, and we refused to miss a show, sometimes attending two in a single day. Apparently the actors found it helpful to have us seated in the front row, for if their memory lapsed they had only to glance over to where Paul and I were sitting and, completely unaware that we were doing so, mouthing the words to the entire operetta.

For months following the shows, we would insist on listening to a recording of the performance as we were falling asleep, placing a small tape recorder in the upstairs hallway between our bedrooms and turning up the volume to near-distortion level so we could all hear. Who knows what effect listening to Gilbert and Sullivan operettas *ad*-well-beyond-*nauseam* has on impressionable children, but we did, all of us, grow up to be as silly as we are musical.

Throughout my life, every three to six months or so, a blind man would come to our house to smooth out the air. It wasn't always the same man, but they were all blind, their eyes like marbles lodged at strange angles in their heads. They were also shy and soft-spoken and they all carried the same wide leather bag. In general, my parents' friends were a boisterous lot, people more apt to cackle than titter, so these quiet, blind men with the wide leather bags were a rare curiosity for me. I was both fascinated and frightened by them.

They would sit alone in the living room, sounding squiggly lines into the air and then gradually working out all the kinks. Sitting at the grand piano with its long lid raised high, the internal harp of wooden felted hammers and coiled metal strings exposed, the blind men would play the same notes over and over and over again, reaching into the quivering belly of the piano with their small wooden instruments and adjusting the corresponding pegs with slow, creaking precision. When they were satisfied, they would move to the next note. It took hours.

Somehow they never got bored, though the same cannot be said for my brothers and me, required as we were to *be quiet* for the duration of the piano tuning and inclined as we were to stray to the rabble-rouser end of the behaviour spectrum whenever silence was requested. Often we were sent outside, a relief in itself, for the act of tuning involves feeling around in the dissonance for the space where the note sings free, and it is not a euphonic exercise.

In fact it's agonizingly tedious. Except if you're blind, I concluded.

Eventually, an unfamiliar car would arrive and take the blind man away. My brothers and I would stream back inside, kicking our boots off in all directions and listening to my mother spinning grand, looping arpeggios from the soundboard like invisible cotton candy.

"There are no bumps in any of the notes anymore!" Flip once commented.

And it was true. After the blind men visited and tinkered with the piano, the air in the house felt all smoothed out.

"Their hearing is more refined," my mother explained when I asked why it was that our piano tuners were always blind. "When we lose one sense, the other senses often compensate by developing more acutely."

"Schools for the blind teach piano tuning because it's a skill the blind can develop well. And it gives them a profession," my father added with a sort of jolly conviction, dusting his rolling pin with flour and rolling out pastry dough on the counter.

The Blind. It was a category I hadn't yet created in my mind. It sounded a bit like *The Catholics* (a term I had learned from my grandmother, who never spoke about them without letting her eyeballs circumnavigate their sockets) or *The Tories* (a group of bald men, in my imagination, with pot-bellies and hair coming out their noses) or *The Bank*, who sometimes called when my dad was at work.

"The Bank called," my mother would say. And I would

picture a long line of people in black hats all dialing our telephone number at once.

"Can The Blind hear as well as Ida?" I asked, sitting on the floor with the black Lab's head in my lap.

"No, no." My father laughed, peeling his dough off the counter and explaining the phenomenon of high frequencies.

My mother sighed and cut in. "It's not really about hearing anyway. When those guys are tuning the piano, they're not really hearing so much as *feeling* the sound."

"Yes, that's true," said my father, sprinkling more flour onto the counter.

Now, hearing my father say (or sing) silly things was certainly not a novelty to me, but normally my mother was more sensible. Tuning the piano by *feeling the sound*? I couldn't find a way to understand that.

So I decided to investigate.

Months passed. I was skipping on the front porch when the strange car arrived. A woman with a flowery orange dress that looked like our kitchen wallpaper led the blind man to the front door. I said "Hi" in that robotic way kids do when they know they're expected to speak, and then I called my mother. Ducked behind the dining room door and peeked through the crack.

The blind man was tall with waxy grey hair that glistened. It was all brushed back so that it looked like those rippling marks that waves leave on sand. (After his last visit my mother had told me that his hair was probably as curly as mine but that he used something called *Brylcreem* to "tame it down." Excited by the phrase *tame it down*, I had gone straight to the bathroom and applied some of my dad's shaving cream—Brylcreem, shaving cream, what's the difference?—but to my distress, I created more of a frothy-wave-crashing-on-rocks look than the wave-textured-sand look I was after.)

My mother settled the ripply-haired blind man at the grand piano and offered him tea, which he softly declined. He sounded the first note. Slowly, I stepped out from behind the dining room door and began to creep into the living room, freezing several times mid-step when it seemed he had heard me. "Hello?" he called once, his lopsided marbles pointing in my direction, a smile on his face. I held my breath. "Hello there," he said playfully, as though he knew it was me, a child at any rate, not my mother. And for a moment, I wondered if he really was blind; I felt sure he could see me. Maybe he was just *pretending* to be blind so that he could tune pianos.

But eventually he turned back to the piano. I exhaled. A bit louder than I'd hoped. (I'd developed asthma, so often wheezed when I breathed.) And he returned to his tools, playing octaves over and over again, drawing up the sound from below, adjusting, re-sounding, adjusting. Until he was satisfied. Then he moved on. I watched him carefully but couldn't find any evidence that he was "feeling the sound." He just seemed to be listening.

I decided to get closer. With what I felt to be the stealth of a professional spy, I lowered myself to the ground, crawling along the soft fringe of the oriental carpet until I was directly beneath the soundboard of the piano. I did not have a plan as such (many professional spies do not), but as I crouched there I became aware of a tingling in my back as the blind man played.

I closed my eyes. And there they were: all those notes, underneath my skin all this time. Resonating in my body as though I were the piano and my ribs the strings. I folded myself down over my thighs and plugged my ears with my fingers. The notes were still there, even stronger than before. Like a thousand purring cats all over me.

I stayed so long I fell asleep, my cheek hot against the carpet when I awoke. From the open window, I could hear a game of kick-the-can starting up in the backyard with some neighbours, so I got to my hands and knees and crawled out of the living room, down the back hallway and out through the flap of Ida's doggie door, until I was safely outside.

I never spoke to anyone about "feeling the sound." It was a discovery that I kept to myself, perhaps my first exploration into the sanctuary of solitude. Whatever it was, music danced into me in a new way that day. I never listened to it the same way again.

The forests and fields at the end of the road soon became my roaming ground and I delighted in walking through them alone, and for hours. Those moments are castings of light across my memory, sparkles of ever-dancing details, impossible to grab at or isolate. What I remember most is that I would hum. And that I felt as much a part of the place as a note to a song.

When I snapped a stalk of tall dry grass between my fingers, the reedy crack would register in my knuckle. Lying on my back, my skull like a mossy cobble in the mud, I would feel whorls of clouds drift through my chest, swelling and shape-shifting across my heart. Crickets rang in my cheekbones, and the calls of cardinals plucked the tips of my ribs. My chapped lips were the peeling bark of the birch tree, its branches tall limbs I would grow into. And the garter snake that once slithered into the cove of my neck as I lay in a spray of ferns became, in that moment, a ringlet of my own hair.

I didn't know I was absorbing the language of place, just as an infant does not consciously train in the dialect of his parents. He simply listens, babbles back, and becomes part of the verbal geography. Similarly when apprenticing in the particular pitch of spruce, the tone of grackle and granite, weasel, aster and snow, we effortlessly tune into the surrounding chorus and grow up with the anthem of the land.

Only when I grew up and began to look for a home beyond my own did I notice that while I resonated with other places, I did not seem to *contain* their resonance. I could learn the language of a country, yes, eat its foods, partake of its ways, wear the fabric of its clothes, but I would live in these new places with a hollowness I found difficult to name. Its leaves were not connected to my skin, I would say; or, its winds did not contain the flavour of my sleep.

For comfort, I would lower myself down the well of memory into the body of that child, the one lying on her back in an August meadow with a black-eyed Susan blossoming between her toes, one arm crooked under a mop of muddy curls, and the elegy of a mourning dove blowing sound rings across an infinite sky.

DOGS AND SEX

One day I came home from school to learn that Ida (diarrhea dog who had, by then, increased her repertoire of pleasing habits to include: drooling into my grandmother's shoes after she'd slipped them off to play cards, and snapping at neighbourhood children) had been taken off to that mythical place known as A Farm. She would be happier there, my mother said. Besides, my asthma was triggered partly by dogs. Then, adding insult to injury, she added that we should be happy she went to such a nice place. I wept bitterly.

The following day, a small white Bichon Frisé arrived. His face was a 360-degree fan of frizzy, hypoallergenic hair. Instantly, I fell in love with him—Sebastian, my comrade in curls—and decided to believe that Ida was romping happily on her Farm and that we were all better off for the new arrangement.

Sebastian was such a hit that soon we acquired another Bichon, Cinnamon, and the springy pair took it upon themselves to become sex education instructors for my brothers and me. First Cinnamon went into heat, prompting my mother to rush out to Sears and purchase padded underwear called training pants, normally used for toddlers, that she styled for a dog by cutting a hole in the back for Cinnamon's tail and a little one in the crotch for the pee. Cinnamon pranced around in variations of that getup for weeks, while Sebastian lost all interest in me—we had been inseparable until then—panting and throwing himself at doors to be with her. I sobbed, feeling a combination of rejection and disgust at his loss of dignity—emotions

I would find myself revisiting with a number of other males later in life.

About six months later, Cinnamon heated up again, but this time we were told that Sebastian would mate her. (Eight-year-old Flip's puzzling comment when he saw the bright red extension of Sebastian's penis was "That's what I need!") The dogs' backyard copulation was the most exciting thing that had happened around our house for a while and my mother didn't discourage us from watching nature in action. My brothers and I giggled and pointed at the humping for the first few minutes, but the post-coital panting and bum-to-bum attachment was so horrendous that it turned me off sex for much of the ensuing decade.

A few weeks after the unromantic union, Cinnamon's body began to fill, her teats swelling underneath her until one evening she moved into an almost hypnotic state, growing purposeful and uncannily focused. My mother helped her into the bed she had prepared and we all gathered around, staying up well into the night, thrilled by the exciting vigil. Cinnamon yelped as the first translucent ball emerged from her body and it was by far the best magic trick I had ever seen. My mother reached over and pinched open the thin sac that encased the puppy's body, peeling the membrane from its face.

From the tiniest mouth I could ever have imagined, I was taught that breath is life.

The summer I turned ten, my father decided that we should celebrate the event with a reading of *Anne of Green Gables*. I was an avid reader by then, devouring books as fast as my parents could put them in front of me, but my father's gift was a *reading* of the book, aloud and together.

He began the ritual by baking Gratin Dauphinoise, a Julia Child recipe that normally calls for white potatoes, but for which my father substituted the red potatoes my mother had brought back from a trip she had taken with her mother and sister to Prince Edward Island that summer. It was the rich, red sandstone and soil of Prince Edward Island that was responsible for the colour of the potatoes, my father explained excitedly as he served up plates of light pink Gratin.

"So was Anne's food always pink?" I asked, picking through the sludge of milky, cheesy potato slices and trying to get inspired to taste it.

Dad laughed. "She probably ate her fair share of potatoes," he replied, scraping away at the sides of the baking dish where a buttery crust of potato was stuck. "But there wouldn't have been any such thing as 'French cooking' in Prince Edward Island back in those days."

I smiled and nodded, silently wishing that there wasn't any such thing as French cooking in Peterborough, Ontario, in *these* days either. But I brought a forkful of gooey pink potatoes to my mouth, chewed cautiously, and was pleasantly surprised by the flavour. *Anne of Green Gables* was getting off to a good start after all.

Once I was all ready for bed—washed, brushed, in my nightgown and under the covers—I was to call out, "Daddy, I'm ready to start reading!" And just as he had done a few months earlier with Paul (with the dreadful-sounding book *Kidnapped* by Robert Louis Stevenson), my dad would lie down on my bed and begin reading, just to me. I coveted it as the privilege it was.

From the beginning, I loved everything about Green Gables: the gossipy neighbour Mrs. Rachel Lynde, sweet Matthew Cuthbert, the feistiness of Anne herself, her spunk and audacity, her untameable nature and godforsaken hair. My father loved it all too, particularly the descriptions of landscapes and sunsets, which sometimes prompted him to stop reading, sigh, and say, "Oh, wasn't that *wonderful*," before carrying on to the next sentence. But our favourite chapter of all was "Matthew Insists on Puffed Sleeves," in which Anne's adoptive father Matthew defies his more practical sister Marilla and sneaks into town to buy Anne the dress she had always dreamed of: one with extravagant puffed sleeves.

Anne took the dress and looked at it in reverent silence. Oh, how pretty it was—a lovely soft brown gloria with all the gloss of silk; a skirt with dainty frills and shir-rings; a waist elaborately pintucked in the most fashion-able way, with a little ruffle of filmy lace at the neck. But the sleeves—they were the crowning glory! Long elbow cuffs, and above them two beautiful puffs divided by rows of shirring and bows of brown-silk ribbon.

My father and I swooned about that dress for weeks afterwards, imagining the dreaminess of the long elbow cuffs and the dainty frills, the great big puffs at the shoulders and how magnificent they would feel.

"Maybe I should buy you a dress with puffed sleeves for Christmas!" he suggested one night, and I fell asleep with my hands clasped under my chin, asking God (in true *Anne of Green Gables* fashion) for exactly that. In any colour but brown.

My dad and I continued reading right up to the penultimate chapter, "The Reaper Whose Name Is Death." I was lying on my back with my eyes closed, imagining the story, as I always did, when dear, sweet Matthew, who had been so kind to Anne every day of her life, suddenly dropped like a sack of PEI potatoes in the doorway, right before Anne's very eyes. My stomach went hot. I squeezed my eyes tightly, hoping that he had just fainted. "Please let the name of death not be Matthew," I whispered to myself.

Alas.

"'Anne looked at the still face and there beheld the seal of the Great Presence,'" Dad read solemnly.

I felt tears gathering under my closed eyes. My dad continued, clearing his throat as he read, faltering uncharacteristically over words and lines, having to go back and repeat certain passages.

"'When the calm night came softly down over Green

Gables the old house was hushed and tranquil. In the parlour lay Matthew Cuthbert in his coffin . . . *ahhhem* . . . his long grey hair framing his pleasant . . . *sorry* . . . his placid face on which there was a little kindly smile as if he but slept, dreaming pleasant dreams. There were . . . *ahhhem* . . . there were flowers about him, sweet old-fashioned flowers which his mother had planted in the bridal homestead . . . *sorry* . . . in the homestead garden in her bridal days and for which Matthew had always had a secret, wordless love. Anne had gathered them and brought them to him, her anguished, tearless eyes burning . . . in her white face. It was the last . . . *the last* . . . thing she could do for him . . .'"

Then his voice went all gurgly. I opened my eyes and turned towards him. His face was wet, the open manila pages of the book speckled with tears.

"You're crying!" I laughed, pulled suddenly out of the story by the shock of it. It might have been the first time I had seen my father cry. "Hey, everyone, Daddy's crying!" I called out teasingly. "Daddy's crying because Matthew Cuthbert just died!" I heard Flip jump out of his bed, but by the time he came running into my room, Dad had shut the book and stood up. "It's just a book!" I called out, laughing and teasing him again.

Dad wiped his face and laid the book on my dresser, not laughing at all. Which made me feel suddenly sick.

"I was just kidding!" I said. "Let's finish reading!"

Flip raced out of the room and down the hall to Paul's room. "Daddy started crying from reading *Anne of Green Gables*!" he called out, proud to be the first boy to get the funny news.

I didn't hear Paul's response. I only saw my dad leave the room.

We never finished *Anne of Green Gables*. Over the next few evenings, I tried to convince Dad to read me the final chapter, but he apologized and said he just couldn't.

"It's too sad," he would say, giving me a little hug. "And then you'll tease me for crying."

So I put the book on my shelf and went on with other things. Other books. All of which I read silently to myself. And one day I was doing just that, reading a book at the kitchen table, when something became clear to me.

My dad was standing at the counter, alternately flouring his rolling pin and rolling out pastry dough, and I was watching him fondly, knowing that some delicious tart would await us at the end of his labour-intensive preparations. I had looked up from my book—*The Secret Garden*, my mother's favourite—and it dawned on me for the first time that my dad was an orphan (albeit an adult one). Both of his parents had died before I was born. And his father would have died, I calculated, when he was about the same age Anne was when Matthew Cuthbert died. There might have been flowers at my dad's father's funeral, maybe even *sweet old-fashioned flowers which his mother had planted in the homestead garden in her bridal days and for which his father had always had a secret, wordless love.*

My dad's tears hadn't been only for Matthew Cuthbert, I realized, my mouth sour with regret, but for his own father, who had died when he was just a boy.

Dad lifted the pastry from the counter, laid it into his French ceramic scalloped-edge tart dish and cut away the dough that hung over the edge. I sat watching him, feeling terribly, sickeningly sorry, but I couldn't bring myself to say a word. I could only watch how focused he was as he primped the tart's edge. In that moment, with his apron covered in flour, his shirt sleeves rolled up, his hands mottled with dough, he was suddenly not just my father, but a person. Someone fragile and full of feelings, someone I had never entirely known, whose life extended far beyond my own.

GYMNASTICS AND STRESS FRACTURES

My father began to spend increasing amounts of time away, even sharing an apartment with some friends in the city of Toronto, where he went to do research for the book he was writing on the Liberal Party of Canada. I thought little of this arrangement, assuming it to be just another way in which humans were similar to dogs: the females tending to the pups while the males sniffed around at the world, lingering and peeing in the places they found most interesting.

I was also unfazed by my father's absences because I had fallen in love. With gymnastics.

For as many hours as I could manage at home and three to four times per week at the local gymnasium, I dedicated myself to the sport: balancing on beams, swinging from bars, creating "floor" routines on the back lawn, doing back-walk-overs across the living room, the splits while watching television, twirls while waiting for my toast to pop, vaults over picnic tables. Nadia Comăneci, the great Romanian gymnast and sweetheart of the 1976 Montreal Olympics, had inspired me to turn myself into a leaping, twisting, tumbling sprite.

I covered the walls of my bedroom in collages created from hundreds of photographs I'd snipped from newspapers and sports magazines of Nadia in various poses and contortions. Her fourteen-year-old body was strong, limber, infallible; her face spoke of resolve and guts. She was the first thing I looked at in the morning, the point of reference I used throughout the day, and the person I was determined to become.

Nadia had scored the first "perfect 10" in gymnastics history and after poring over her routines and photographs with a hypercritical eye, I subjected myself to the same scrutiny. Good was not good enough; excellent wasn't either. Lots of gymnasts were excellent—Teodora Ungureanu was second only to Nadia, but who's ever heard of Teodora Ungureanu? No, in order to stand out, in order to win, to be rewarded, admired and celebrated, I would have to be perfect.

But my attempts-to-emulate-Nadia phase was as doomed as my wannabe-Laura-Ingalls phase of several years earlier. For one, I smiled too much; couldn't help it. No steely look of determination for me. My curls made the gymnast-ponytail look comical (again, think horizontal). But most crucially, I was too old. By the time I joined the Peterborough Gymnastics Club, I was (the near-decrepit age of) ten; Nadia had started at five. While she had trained eight hours a day, the most I could register for was eight per week. Still, I tried. Ten points for effort. Too much effort, as it turned out, for I trained so hard and incessantly that by the time I was twelve I had developed debilitating lower back pain.

After a few inconclusive appointments with our family doctor, my mother took me to a sports doctor in Toronto. Initially I felt quite proud to have an appointment with a sports doctor—it was the kind of thing, I felt, that Nadia would have done—but a bone scan revealed a stress fracture in one of my lower vertebrae. In addition to a period of two to three months of rest, the specialist prescribed a daily diet of twelve—count 'em: twelve—aspirins per day. I was a wisp of a thing, well under a hundred pounds, so the regimen was almost guaranteed to blot out my back pain, in addition, no doubt, to most other sensations.

Directly after my appointment, my mother and I went to have dinner with my dad at his city apartment. I told him all about my stress fracture, and then he and my mom discussed it a bit while I chatted and laughed with my dad's roommate, Tom, who was friendly and lots of fun. I don't remember what dinner was like, but afterwards, Tom and my mom joked about how messy my dad was in the kitchen, and then she said, "Well, we don't want to keep you from the pleasure of doing the dishes!" and we got going. At the door, Dad thanked us for coming, Mom thanked him for dinner, we all hugged, and then my mom and I drove back to Peterborough.

My Acetylsalicylic Acid Period was not my happiest. I missed gymnastics. I missed the natural joy that comes with being so active and passionately engaged. After a few months of rest, my back was no better (I was still in chronic pain, despite the aspirin-buzz), and I agreed, reluctantly but resignedly, to give up gymnastics for good.

Briefly, as consolation, I took up ballet, but just as I was beginning to enjoy the classes, I developed the first hint of flesh on my thighs and stomach and felt too fat and old to continue. The back pain would dog me for the rest of my adolescence, but like so many other things, its intensity faded as I grew used to it.

My father had been spending a lot of time away, having taken part of his half-year's sabbatical in Germany. One night, while I was lying on the floor playing with the latest litter of puppies, the telephone rang.

"Hello?" I answered.

"Hi, it's Dad!" he said excitedly, transatlantic telephone calls still an echoey and miraculous venture in those days.

"Oh, hi, I'll get Mom," I said immediately, putting down the phone, calling up the stairs, and lying back down amid the warm kibble-breath of the puppies.

I discovered later that my father was shocked and hurt by my indifference, but I was so accustomed to his extended absences I hadn't even realized that that transatlantic call was the first time we had spoken in three months.

My parents never fought, which isn't to say they didn't disagree or that my father didn't drive my mother "'round the bend," as she used to say, by arriving late to virtually everything (especially concerts, train stations, airports and diaper changes), or by following her down the driveway as she left on a very rare two-week holiday with her mother and sister to say, "I just want to tell you, this comes at a very inconvenient time." Or by leaving his nightly cereal bowl and spoon on the counter in such a way that it left a little milk puddle for her to wipe up every morning. Et cetera.

The only thing I ever heard about my mother that may have driven my father bonkers was the way she clammed up when she was upset and retreated to the family room, where she would close the door, curl up in a rocking chair and listen to Schubert *Lieder*. For hours. If my father pursued her and asked what was wrong, the answer was always "Nothing." So, they did not yell at each other or even raise their voices, and with what felt like logic, I thought that meant that Everything Was Fine.

Paul was reading books about Churchill, little white dogs were running around in bloodied training pants, my mother was running around good-naturedly from marathon races to piano to dishwasher, and though Flip briefly replaced hat bacon with finger bacon (hot dogs) and *tried* cheese, he quickly reverted to his signature diet, we all exhaled, and life returned to normal again.

When my father returned from his sabbatical in Germany, he busied himself in the garden, as he did every summer, his bare back browning in the sun as he meandered and crouched along the edges of his elaborate, curving flowerbeds, his shirt flung over his head like a floppy bonnet. ("Why is your dad wearing a bonnet?" my friend Mary once asked. "Oh," I said, casting a glance at his strange getup, and answering, rather portentously it seems now, "my dad's different; he does things like that.")

My father was forever trying to engage me in examining a flower—"Look at the way this one blooms so audaciously!"— and I was forever bored with all the blooming. When he wasn't gardening, listening to music or fussing over a recipe from *Gourmet* magazine, he was involved with life at the university or life in Toronto; I never really distinguished between the two.

On rare and special occasions, my brothers and I went with him to Toronto, although normally we went one at a time as that made for unique, individually tailored adventures. My own father–daughter weekends included things like *The Nutcracker* ballet or eating fancy cakes in restaurants with embossed menus and handsome waiters who asked, "And for the young lady?"—meaning me!

But most of the time, I stayed in Peterborough and led an ordinary, contented, little life: I had good friends, enjoyed school, read books, took up the flute. And whenever I had the urge, I would walk in long afternoon light through the fields at the end of our road to a hilltop with a view of spiral hay bales and a barn.

Life was comfortable, simple and mostly predictable. I had no reason to believe it would ever be otherwise.

I remember the night my mother told me.

I was twelve, though I cannot place the feeling of that age. Thinking back to the moment the floor cracked, I was like a fledgling bird: transparent skin clinging to bone and an exposed throat, wide and voiceless, wings folded tight to my body.

The following day I would step onto an airplane alone and fly to Frankfurt to spend a month with the family of a German girl I had met through a gymnastics exchange. I had stopped doing gymnastics by then, but I was excited at the prospect of adventure. I was also nervous, I imagine, although that emotion is something I have stapled to the memory rather than something that calls itself up on its own. All that I truly remember is sitting in the kitchen perched on a stool with two fold-down steps that I gripped with my toes and kept lifting and dropping to the floor. *Creak creak creak—crash.* My mother was unloading the dishwasher, her eyes pulled tight with annoyance at both the continual slamming of the steps and my persistent questions:

"Will Dad be at the airport tomorrow to see me off?"

Creak creak creak—crash.

"Why doesn't he come home very much anymore?"

Creak creak creak—crash.

"I don't see why he has to have an apartment in Toronto . . ."

Creak creak creak—crash.

"Well," my mother began, clicking three brown and white cereal bowls together and stacking them in the cupboard, then standing for an extra few moments and running her hand along the counter. "There are a lot of things about Dad that you don't know."

"Like what?" I asked in the tone of a challenge, a schoolyard taunt, with saucy shoulders and a raised chin, the way I would speak to a girl who claimed to know something embarrassing about me that she was threatening to broadcast to the class.

Or, no.

That wasn't it at all. It was more of a mealy-mouthed squeak, the way someone might talk if they felt that the flight of their voice into the air might collapse the roof.

"Like what?"

For a long time she said nothing, just walked back to the dishwasher, pulled up the cutlery basket and set it on the counter with her back to me. I watched her gather all the knives together and place them—*clink clink clink*—into the drawer. Then the forks, her strong pianist's fingers folding around the tines and pulling the utensils up, one by one.

It was many years before I stopped to wonder how she might have felt as she drew those forks out of that blue plastic mesh basket—one . . . at . . . a . . . time—and decided what to say. That moment has come to me many times along with memories of that dishwasher, the one that seemed to vomit grit all over the dishes as it washed them, bits of black sand we would pry loose with our fingernails from cups and spoons before we used them. If she was around, my brothers and I would always blame my mother for the silt—*Maawwm, there's crud on this bowl!*—as though she'd deliberately sprinkled sand on the clean dishes before putting them away. How she kept herself from curling her arm and Frisbee-ing the half-clean plates at our heads is still beyond me.

So I have thought of the dishwasher and that stool, its orange flower-patterned seat and the two rubber-matted steps we would flip down to climb up and reach the cereal shelf. And I have thought of that twelve-year-old girl in her nightie, the feeling of being perched, and of anticipating her first flight alone the next day.

But only now, more than thirty years later, do I find myself staring out at overgrown grass and the whiteness of a tired sky, recalling the moment and wondering, for the first time, what my mother may have felt as she decided what to say.

"Do you remember the time you came back from Toronto and told me that Dad had taken you to a gay bar?" she asked, pulling out a bundle of spoons and placing them, with excruciating gentleness, in the drawer.

Our kitchen floor. That spongy beige linoleum with the brown swiggly patterns designed for some purpose utterly unrelated to aesthetics. I burrowed into it, the brute ugliness of it, my eyes digging frantically for a way out of the conversation, the room, the fire that began to fill my body. I recall pulling myself into a ball, drawing my knees up under my sheer white nightgown until it threatened to split down the middle. That terrifying and exhilarating sensation of near evisceration. And how, underneath the threat of explosion, my stomach tightened into such a small knot that it virtually disappeared.

For years.

Sitting there with my toes curled over the stool's edge, I rewound my mind to the phrase and replayed it: *Dad took me to a gay bar.*

Why had I said that? Anyway, I hadn't meant it like *that*. But why did I say "a gay bar"? It was just a fancy restaurant we had gone to, with a handsome waiter and a chandelier. Had Dad called it a gay bar? If he had, he was probably joking. Maybe he meant "gay" as in "happy," because it *was* actually quite a happy restaurant. Happy restaurant, gay bar. Same thing! What a mistake!

That entire string of denial spun through my mind in a few seconds and then snapped, because the moment I looked up, my mother's expression said it all.

There was no mistake. And there was nothing happy about this.

I don't remember what was said in what order, but I do remember my mother concluding that it wasn't going to be easy for my father. That being gay meant "a lonely life." Which made the whole thing even more impossible to understand. Why would he want that? Why would he want to have a lonely life in Toronto when he could just be here with us?

I didn't understand what being gay meant, aside from knowing that it was Very Bad News and had to do with boys kissing boys. Which was gross. There were no gay references in my world in those days, and I had no context for that word at all. No one said *He's gay* other than as an insult, and I knew very well that there was nothing at school or in the neighbour-hood—*nothing*—worse than that.

How could my dad suddenly be the worst thing there was? How could that possibly, possibly be?

I remember crying a lot and feeling freezing cold, even though it was the middle of summer. Neither of my brothers was home—were they at summer camp?—so the house had a huge emptiness about it that night; just my mother and me under a bell jar. I don't remember any of the questions I asked or what else my mother said. Except that towards the end of the evening, just before we made our dazed way to bed, she took a deep breath and said, "And do you know what else?"

What *else*? Oh God. How could there possibly be an *else*?

Then she told me: Virginia, my former gymnastics coach, was also gay (the word *lesbian* hadn't arrived yet in Peterborough). And, as if that wasn't enough, she and Mrs. Harper, the mother of my fellow gymnast and friend Julie, had "just run off together."

I was greatly relieved by this news, even though I had no idea (again) what any of it meant. For some reason, I had been instantly terrified that the *else* was that my mother was gay too. Why not? At that point, anything seemed possible. But no, *thank God thank God thank God*, it was only Virginia. *And* Mrs. Harper. The two of them clad in blue jeans with the cuffs rolled up (I imagined), skipping hurriedly through fields of tall grasses, hand in hand, "running off together." Why, or to where, I could not imagine.

I wish I could say that I felt sad for my friend Julie, but I'm not sure I had the capacity to feel sorry for anyone but myself at that moment. It was more likely that I got a small jolt of pleasure from Julie's misfortune, that seductive sting of glad-it's-not-me delight that drives gossip mills and tabloids. For I was definitely comforted to know that there were other parents going off and doing unimaginably awful things, and heartened to hear that my life could have been a whole lot worse. Until then, it had never occurred to me that mothers could leave home; as far as I was concerned, they *were* home. So at least it wasn't my *mother* who was running off to be gay; that would have been like the whole house collapsing. My dad running off to be gay just felt like a bomb had gone off in my stomach.

At the airport the next day, I clutched my ticket to Frankfurt so forcefully that by the time I checked in, the smudged lettering was almost illegible. My mother was there, as always, and my father arrived late, as always, just as I was about to walk through the customs gate, a series of doors and officials that felt menac-ing; I couldn't imagine how I would get past them all without bursting from the pressure of the tears and terror I held inside.

I don't remember the actual goodbye, only my father's quick step as he arrived (from his Toronto apartment) and his jolly manner, the way he grabbed my mother playfully around the waist, and how she flinched. Steeled herself and tried to be good-natured. Albeit stiffly.

No doubt my mother regretted the previous evening's dis-closure. It hadn't been planned and the timing was, obviously, pretty dreadful. She had found out about my dad only a few months earlier, so maybe her judgment was off. Whatever it was, I felt completely disoriented even before boarding the plane.

The memory crunches at this point, the way our old 8mm films used to at the end of a reel. Ours were among the first generation of home movies, and oh did we love them, my brothers and I. Nothing, but nothing, could compete with watching silent stilted scenes of ourselves at various stages of development. Our greatest shrieks of delight came on those evenings when my father would clap his hands together and suggest that we set up the projector.

There he is: Paul, at age three, trying his hand at conducting with my father's baton, a look of acute seriousness falling across his face as he waves the stick around him, flipping the pages of the music score with great concentration, but backwards, following various lines with his finger, his intensity and passion building (pure child mimicry here), tongue curled over his lip, until he is conducting so furiously that it looks as though the baton is about to take flight. Hilarious every time.

Or precious moments such as my potty training outside a crumbling stone house in southern France, Paul proudly marching around the bowl of urine in his Buckingham Palace–guard costume while I waddle towards the camera with a smile of self-satisfaction. I could have watched the scene a thousand times. Especially for a child, it is pleasing to see proof that one was once effortlessly adorable.

There are summers at cottages with untannable English friends, watermelon-seed spitting contests and unhappy babies in playpens. Unintentional shots of my grandmother's shins as she sits on the sofa watching us on Christmas morning the year she gives us the Fisher-Price castle—could our mouths have stretched wider with joy? There is Judy, the skinny English nanny who lived with us for a year, tossing grapes up into the air with my mother, the two of them catching the fruits in their mouths with great comical self-congratulations each time a little green orb makes it through the drawbridge of their teeth. My brothers and me (aged seven, six and three) marching angrily the length of the kitchen with placards that read WE WANT TO STAY UP FOR THE PARTY! and ERLY BEDTIME — NO WAY! while my mother and her sister sit off to the side giggling into their hands. Aunt Sally, ever the sophisticate, posing seductively in a doorway exhibiting the uncommon talent of crossing her eyes and making circles with only the right one. Flip posing solemnly with Ida the black Lab, Flip in his best shirt and Ida in a headband of ribbons, just after his announcement that he intended, a bit later in life, to marry her. My father dancing around in the backyard, his hands flitting about like butterflies, urging us to join him. His enthusiasm is visibly contagious and in no time my brothers and I, Flip still a toddler, are delightedly following behind trying to imitate my father's style, wobbling our hips and swirling our hands behind him as he prances around the garden like a fairy.

Oh my.

While foraging for extra blankets at my mother's house one Christmas decades later, Flip and I came across the old projector in her basement and set it up excitedly. We laughed at the same scenes all over again, rose up in our seats and filled in some of the sound effects or details about certain moments that we remembered.

And then came the *let's all dance like pixies!* scene: my father leaping about, actually *pointing* his toes as he lifted them off the ground.

"Uh, that would be Dad," Flip acknowledged, raising his eyebrows and rubbing his beard. As my father's nimble body frolicked along the white basement wall, Flip's shoulders began to shake. Mine followed. And by the time the film spun to a finish and slapped its loose end round and around the projector, we were both leaning into each other, laughing uproariously.

Uh. That would be Dad.

"Did you ever have any idea?" people often ask. "Did you ever wonder if he was gay?"

Fair questions, I suppose. The crème brûlée and all. His preference for gambolling over gambling. Opera in the streets, yes yes.

But no.

As a Canadian child of the 1970s, no more did I suspect my father of being a closeted dandy than I harboured suspicions of my rice-enamoured mother being secretly Chinese. While it's all mainstream sitcom nowadays, at that time the kind of thing my father was up to simply *was not done.* Except a few hours away, in a place called Toronto, where although one still might have been hard-pressed to find a drink on Sundays, if one knew where to go (and for a time the police did not) one could find a gay bathhouse.

Or a gay bar.

Though that was not, in fact, what my dad and I had visited during the notable father–daughter weekend that my mother would later refer to. What we had gone to was a restaurant, such a novelty to me then that it might as well have been a bar. It was a pleasant place, bright and fancy with an ample array of ornamental flowers. There was even, to my father's felicity, a chandelier. Sitting there on a puffy vinyl seat reading an embossed white menu with a red ribbon draped down the middle, I felt very much the princess, and happily-ever-after-ly so.

The tables were long and set quite close together, so in my recollection we were soon chatting with two men seated along the wall, as well as an older gentleman at the end of our table. It might well have been a pickup joint, a safe place for queers to get quietly acquainted, but if anything like that was going on, I was unaware of it. I only remember everyone being exceptionally friendly, sweet and attentive to me, and witty, full of jokes and giggles. When we stepped onto the sidewalk of a grey, early winter day, I recall turning to my father and exclaiming, "I liked going there!" As well as the dewy-eyed delight on his face as he said, "Well, maybe I could take you there again sometime!" Then he threaded his arm through mine and skipped me all the way to the subway.

Could one of the men have ribbed him at some point, some innocuous joke about bringing his daughter to a gay bar? I no longer remember. It is said that children know everything, every unspoken subtlety that passes through the lives of their parents, and I suspect that may be so. But the only thing I know for certain is that I took the Greyhound bus back to Peterborough, walked to our house on Merino Road and flopped into the kitchen, where I found my mother sweeping. And to her then-standard question, So what did you and Dad do in Toronto? I leaned my elbow over the back of a chair and responded, "Oh, he took me to a gay bar."

Creak creak creak—crash.

Germany was a well-ordered blur. Poppyseed-speckled *Brötchen* for breakfast, hairy-armpitted women, criss-cross fairy-tale houses, tours of cathedrals that all but drained the blood from my body, hundreds of games of backgammon with my host family's fun-loving father, an intestineful of Wiener schnitzel, beds that needed to be unrolled every night in my "host sister" Jutta's terminally tidy room, and a feverish insomnia that would have me huddled on the windowsill looking down on dark, empty cobblestone streets scribbling into the diary my dad had given me at the airport as an early birthday present.

I had never really kept a journal before, certainly nothing of any substance, but I began to write in that little blue diary because I thought I would burst if I didn't. So many questions churned within me that at any given moment I could have leaned over and vomited: hundreds of words spattering out of my mouth onto those immaculate German sidewalks.

> *Fag. Faggot. Poofter. Queen. Pansy. Gay. Why??? What does it* mean*?? Does Dad love Paul and Flip and not me? Does he still love Mom? Does he still like her* at least*? Can he still live with us? Does she hate him? Will they have to get divorced? How are we going to keep everyone from* finding out*???*

No doubt they found me strange, Jutta's kind and welcoming family. Sleeping half the day, picking at my breaded lamb with sullen ingratitude, incapable of appreciating their hospitality or enjoying myself for more than a few minutes at a time. I remember weeping on the telephone to my mother the day I woke up convinced I had cancer in my knees. Or wishing I did, not sure which. I seemed unable to decide whether I hoped I was dying or was petrified that I was. In either case, I was desperate for some kind of reassurance from my mother.

On the last night of my six-week stay, the Thiemanns threw me a beautiful if undeserved thirteenth birthday party with all the local girls and their families. A few days after that, I packed my navy blue fake leather suitcase full of souvenir coins, pins, leotards and postcards, along with a head full of the German words for things like potato salad—*Kartoffelsalat*—and butterfly—*Schmetterling!*—and flew home.

At the airport, I was thrilled to see both my parents waiting for me. All the way to the parking lot, I bubbled over with stories and proudly recited a joke I had memorized in German, a language they both spoke a bit. My father was overjoyed by my state, exclaiming that clearly Germany had been very *stimulating* for me and wasn't that wonderful! My dad often used that word, *stimulating*—Travel was so *stimulating*! Wasn't that concert *stimulating*!—but all of a sudden the word made me squirm. I saw my mom roll her eyes, but we all said goodbye civilly, my dad getting into his car and explaining that he was staying in Toronto (clearly a more *stimulating* city than Peterborough) and he'd see me soon. My mom and I got into her car and drove back to Merino Road.

A few days later, I came downstairs to find Dad in his

French silk pyjamas reading the newspaper in the kitchen. We chatted briefly, even phlegmed our way through a few words of German, until he began fidgeting with the paper and said sternly, nervously, but with impeccable grammar, "Mom told me that before you left for Germany, you and she had an important chat."

Quickly, I reached for the Harvest Crunch. *Plink plink plink*. A tumble of glazed oats falling into my bowl. Lungs like limp socks on a clothesline. No breath, no breath.

"Yeah," I said with a stab at teenage aloofness. "She told me, but I don't care."

Lie number one.

Of thousands.

Paul already knew.

Dad had told him a few months earlier when they were having one of their father–son weekends at my dad's apartment in Toronto, his time at home having become increasingly rare since his sabbatical the previous year. Paul was quiet for a bit, but shortly after that he brightened up and asked if they were still going out for Chinese food. Which they did and had a wonderful time. That's what Dad told me.

Chinese food?

Quiet for a bit and then Chinese food?

I looked down at my bowl of Harvest Crunch, the oatballs swelling out into the splosh of now-syrupy, off-colour milk, the lumpy mass looking like something I'd already eaten and brought up. I could barely lift the spoon to my mouth. How on earth did Paul manage Chinese food?

I have no memory of what we said next, but it was no doubt the verbal equivalent of covering up an unsightly stain on the carpet by looking towards the ceiling. I believe he offered to answer any questions I might have. And all I could think of was sitting in that windowsill in Jutta's room, and how I had been so frightened that someone would see the words I had spent the night scribbling into my journal that the moment I finished writing I shredded every page into pieces and ate them.

Nope, no questions.

Although there were a few. Like, how can you choose to live in that sleazy, graffiti-covered apartment building in concrete-ville Toronto when you could just stay here in our perfectly nice Peterborough house with all those gardens you spent years fluffing up?

Or, why can't you keep being normal during the week and just go to Toronto to be gay on the weekends? (I couldn't have known that they had been trying that, he and my mother, but the obvious snag to the arrangement—namely, Married Life As Ludicrous Hoax—was making it impossible to continue.)

Or, can't you at least come back and cook once in a while? We could have one day a week when we all eat soufflé.

Or, what's so wrong with everything the way it is? I thought we were all having a pretty good time.

But I didn't ask him anything. I just wanted the conversation to end. As did my dad, it seemed, for I had never before seen him so uncomfortable: nervously clearing his throat, fidgeting with the newspaper, running his hands down the sides of his pyjamas as though he were trying to rub something off. He may have tried to say a few reassuring things, but I have no memory of what these might have been.

Years later, I learned that Paul's reaction had not, in fact, been "quiet for a bit" and then out for Chinese food, as had been recounted to me that watershed morning. Perhaps my dad had wanted to spare me my brother's pain, or maybe he had hoped that making Paul out to be such a take-it-in-stride kind of a guy might inspire me to similar heights. Whatever the reason, I remember feeling that the bar had been set quite high (far above the realm of tears, blubbering and pleading, certainly), and that I had better fling myself over it as best I could.

But thirty-two years later, a national newspaper contacted my dad and me for a story they were doing about children of gay parents. We agreed to the interview, and soon after sat together in the living room of Dad's Wedgwood blue house, the soft-spoken reporter asking a series of standard questions, prodding, in that unapologetically intimate way reporters can, into some of the most private moments of our lives.

"And how was it telling your children you were gay?"

Dad inhaled deeply and pressed back into the sofa. I looked at him, freshly seventy-five and looking fit but undeniably like the grandfather he was.

"Well, it wasn't easy, of course. I remember that after I told my eldest son when he was thirteen, he sat in a corner of my apartment, crying and crying," Dad said.

I sat beside him, stunned. "I thought he just wanted to go out for Chinese food."

Dad looked puzzled. "What?"

"You told me he was quiet for a bit and then you went out for Chinese food."

His face held both bewilderment and amusement. "Well, maybe we did. I don't remember. We certainly ate a lot of it in those days. But he was very, very upset for a long time. Watching him crying was one of the most agonizing moments of my life."

As the interview continued, I sat on the sofa flipping through the pages of memory until I came to the scene in question, and rewrote a passage that had never quite read true:

Paul was quiet for a bit, but very quickly he brightened up and asked if they were still going out for Chinese food.

Paul sobbed and sobbed. Watching him crying was one of the most agonizing moments of Dad's life.

The moment I adjusted the memory, I felt a palpable relief. This is what truth does for us.

I crossed into adolescence prosaically. It would embolden my ego to report a fascination for Yeats, an early devotion to Shakespeare or Shostakovich, but alas, my early teenage years saw me reading teen magazines and listening to the Bee Gees. I spent my afternoons wandering alone in the back fields reciting mawkish poetry to wildflowers. Had *ze-ro* interest in smoking or having a toke. Even found swearing offensive. And having spent my early years bouncing bath toys on Paul's stretched scrotum—a game we called Trampoline—or being pinned down while he and Flip both dangled mucilaginous strings of spit over my face or spread their corduroy-wrapped cheeks over my face and farted, I was also cured of any romantic curiosity I might have developed for boys and what it was they went in for. When my body began brewing the hormonal cocktail of puberty and serving it up in two tender nubbles on my chest, my life was still an intensely virginal, vaguely insipid non-event.

The day rust appeared in my underwear (at the embarrassingly advanced age of fourteen), I gathered up my canine-inspired vocabulary and approached my mother in her bedroom, producing the evidence and announcing solemnly, "I think I'm in heat."

Calmly, she said, "Let me get you something for that."

While she disappeared into the bathroom, I remained fixed—terror bolting me to the spot—hoping to God she wasn't going to fix me up with a pair of that padded underwear with a hole cut out for the tail.

It pleases me greatly to say that she did not. Intimacies of that kind were not my mother's forte, however, so she passed me the feminine hygiene products and left me to decipher them alone in the bathroom. The situation was never spoken of again.

Once I had mastered the art of hiding menstruation from the world, I got back to the secret of having a pansy father. What weighed more heavily than anything else was what everyone would *say*. Not to mention the confusion of not understanding what exactly the whole thing meant.

I certainly puzzled over it. Spent the wee hours of a few nights flipping, with a combination of horror and unanticipated titillation, through the copy of *The Joy of Gay Sex* that sat on a bookshelf in Dad's apartment. But once I got a handle on the crude logistics, I discovered that, gay or straight, the maxim is the same: when it comes to our parents' sexual practices, we'd rather not think about the details. And for good reason: they're not meant to be any of our business.

When the initial *Dad-does-THAT?* incredulity wore off, it became clear that my real interest lay not so much in knowing the how or in what position, but in understanding what his being gay meant in practical, day-to-day terms. What it meant to the world, for our family and, more pertinently, what it meant to *me*.

"Don't make a big deal about your father being gay," advised Ron, a friend of my father's and host of the Gay Fathers of Toronto potluck we were attending. Dad had thought it would be nice for me to meet some other gay dads and kids "in my situation," but I just stood there, shocked, watching men's fingers intertwining as they spoke to each other, one man laying his head on another man's shoulder on the sofa.

I didn't want to meet other gay dads or kids in my situation. I wanted a different situation.

But here I was.

Dad's friend Ron wore an earring(!) and spoke with one eyebrow constantly raised, an expression that made him look condescending even when he was trying to be kind. "Being gay is just part of who your father is, so try to think of it as you would anything else about him: he has curly hair, he's a professor, he likes music, he's gay," he said so matter-of-factly I could only nod in agreement.

"He'th the thame perthon he alwayth wath," added Sammy, a leather-clad man who called himself "Ron's lover" (although with his ultra-gay sibilant speech, it sounded more like "Thammy, Ron'th lover"). Thammy leaned forward and took my hand in his. "It'th jutht that you're theeing *more* of your father than ever before," he said, his cheeks rippling around a broad smile.

I nodded again, wanting to yank my icy fingers from his pillow-soft palm and poke both my eyes out.

Four men were giggling on the couch, one of them my father, who was at that moment being tickled by a grey-haired, pot-bellied man with an extravagance of nose hair. An Anglican minister, I later learned. Scattered around the house, playing as though they didn't even *notice*, were kids of all ages.

I escaped to the kitchen, where a round, floral-clothed table held a large ceramic bowl of pesto pasta, a startlingly symmetrical salad made of something called "endive," a tray of melon balls, and crystal glasses filled to a swirled point with chocolate mousse.

I spent the rest of the Gay Fathers of Toronto potluck with a girl my age named Pilar, who had grown up with her father and his "partner" (new word for me), knew things that I did not (endive, for example), and had a confident ease about her, sauntering through the party as though it were a Girl Guides meeting, chatting and joking with the men, men, men. Trailing behind her, I could feel myself resisting, pulling my foot back as it swung out for its next step, mentally turning and scrabbling on the heavy psychic door marked *Innocence*. Making gouge marks down the one marked *Normal Life*.

After the potluck, Dad and I returned to his apartment in St. James Town, a collection of seamy high-rise apartments where—bafflingly—he had chosen to live on the weekends. It was at the edge of Toronto's Gay Village (gay ghetto, in those days), and so home to some colourful characters in full expression.

We got into a graffiti-splattered elevator and just as the doors were closing, a large man wearing a pink tutu, pink tights and a blond wig trotted across the dismal lobby, waving at us to keep the doors open. Which—bafflingly—Dad did. The man greeted us politely (I'm sure I didn't even cough out a hello), and moments later, a few floors up, as he prepared to step off the elevator he waggled his fingers and in a squawky high-pitched voice said, "Toodle-oo!"

"Have a good night," my father replied in a friendly way.

And I remember turning and being quietly astonished that my father would know what to say to a man in a pink tutu who said *toodle-oo*.

As the tutu-clad man stepped out of the elevator, he was greeted by a man in skin-tight white jeans. "Ooooh, look at the shiny drag queen!" he squeaked, giving the tutu a little tug and the man's cheek an affectionate pinch.

The elevator doors closed.

We lurched up ten more floors.

"Dad, what's a drag queen?"

"Oh, that's a man who enjoys dressing up as a woman," Dad answered cheerfully, as though the question had been *What's a cheerleader?* and his answer had been *Oh, that's someone who roots for your team!*

I began to worry. Did he think it was *okay* for men to dress up like women? Why had he explained it so *chirpily*?

The smell of stale feet greeted us as the elevator doors opened again. We walked down the hallway to Dad's apartment and he opened the door with a flourish, singing "Ta-da!" He had just painted the kitchen a strange beige-orange and hoped I would like it.

Dad made dinner while I picked my teeth and lounged awkwardly at the table. Then we got out the cards and played a game of cribbage, Dad all plucky with enthusiasm and me suddenly scared by all his pluckiness. It took me ages to work up the courage, but I wasn't sure I'd be able to get through the night if I didn't ask.

"So, Dad?"

He was busy counting and shifting his cards around. "Yes?" he said without looking up.

"So, I was just wondering . . ." I continued, sounding as blasé as I could, "if maybe you're a drag queen."

Dad laughed. Sort of whooped. Put down his cards and fluttered his hands around as though they were little sparrows, which I did not take as a very good sign. "No, don't worry. I'm not a drag queen. Not all gay men are drag queens."

I could have inflated an air mattress with the breath I exhaled. "So why do they do that? Like, why was that guy wearing a tutu?"

Dad shrugged. "I guess he just finds it kind of fun."

Kind of fun.

I wasn't sure what to do with that explanation.

Decided to pick my cards back up.

Maybe try for a flush.

I can't remember where I used to sleep in that apartment (Dad didn't live there very long), but it might have been on the couch in the main room. Wherever it was, that night I lay awake listening to the traffic, staring at the city lights out the curtainless windows and carving out a slightly different perspective on my situation. Suddenly, there was something worse than being gay. There was being a drag queen. And at least Dad wasn't one of those. In spite of the cars roaring through my head and the strangeness of the apartment, I relaxed slightly, knowing that there were men out there walking around in tutus and saying toodle-oo, and at least my dad was slightly more normal than that.

A RECIPE AND A REVELATION

While divorce was not unheard of in those days, it was uncommon enough, particularly under these circumstances, that acquaintances in Peterborough were left to improvise the recipe for an Appropriate Reaction:

> 1 part indignation, for there was nothing as dissolute as what my father was doing, apparently, especially in *this* kind of town
>
> 5 parts pity, that lumpy ingredient that is such a relief to offload and so back-breaking to receive
>
> 3 parts denial, a highly soluble emotion that gives most situations a pleasingly creamy texture
>
> 10 parts pre-sifted silence, with the neighbourhood taking on a collective strained smile and hush-hush tone, everyone knowing everything but no one actually saying a word about anything.
> Ever.

Which left me wondering.

Did my father now cease to exist to everyone but my brothers and me? Would he keep being part of our lives in secret or would he eventually disappear into some epicene vortex somewhere around the Toronto intersection of Church and Wellesley? What would I say if people eventually asked? Would I need to invent an imaginary heterosexual person called "my dad" and talk about all the great, straight things we did together? What kinds of things did straight fathers engage their daughters in anyway? None of the ones that I knew baked or sang Broadway show tunes over breakfast or went to the ballet or liked shopping. What on earth did these enviable, heterosexual fathers actually *do*?

The only childhood friend I ever told was Jessica Bell. I was fourteen. I had kept the secret to myself for a year, until late one night when we were lounging on the floor of Jessica's basement, sloshing ourselves up with a mickey of rum she kept stashed for such occasions. I had never tried alcohol before, but pretended to be seasoned because I longed to be as confident and grown-up as I saw Jessica to be.

As the spiked Coke poured through me, I felt myself unfurling, my stomach unclenching. The basement pulsed with the high-pitched, chimpanzee-esque chanting of the Bee Gees and I felt cool and sophisticated for the first time in my life. And then the words came out:

"My dad's gay."

There. I'd said it.

Oh my God. I'd *said* it. I'd *said* it. I'd actually fucking *said* it.

Jessica lay beside me, torturously silent.

The panting and squealing of the Bee Gees throbbed around us.

"Get outta town," Jessica eventually said in a tone that meant *stop fooling around*.

"My dad's gay," I said again. (Oh my God, I'd fucking said it *again*!)

More silence.

Until finally she asked, "You mean, like a *fag*?"

I didn't know how to answer that. So I didn't.

"For real? Like . . . he does it with other *guys*?"

I didn't know how to answer that either. Or maybe I just didn't want to answer that.

Jessica shifted her position on the floor. Drank some more. Let another song go by. By the time she spoke again, she was thick-lipped and droopy, the alcohol seeping into all the spaces between the words.

"So . . . is yer mom gonna kick 'im out?"

I shrugged. Had no idea.

"So . . . is it kinda weird t'be around him now or is it just kinda the same?"

I shrugged again. Had no idea.

We both retreated into our respective stupors, letting the primatological disco music dominate the moment.

"Well, I'll still like 'im," Jessica eventually promised. "And I won't tell anyone anything—*honest.*" She tipped more rum into her can of Coke, tucked the bottle back under the sofa and leaned into my ear. "And holy fuck, you think that's bad," she said in a husky whisper. "My dad's been havin' an affair for the last twelve years. He's even got a kid over'n East City that we're not s'posed to know about."

Mr. Bell. Lawyer, school board trustee, pillar of the community.

Once Jessica had poured out the details of her story, we sat on the floor together, blinking in all the new information.

The music ended, leaving the needle of the record player trip-ping—*flumb flumb flumb*—against the label. We sat in the blurry stillness of the basement until Jessica said, "Shit, man. I can't figure out which one of our lives is more fucked up."

"Yeah, I know what you mean," I said, stupefied.

We roped our arms around each other like survivors of a shipwreck and carried each other upstairs. Sitting on the shag carpet of her lacy, pink bedroom—neither of us felt steady enough to sit on her bed—we stared at the ceiling and digested the evening's revelations all over again.

"You know what?" Jessica finally said angrily, kicking through the silence with her signature expression: "Men suck."

In Jessica's mind pretty much everything eventually sucked. School sucked. Summer holidays sucked. Snow sucked. The boy she had liked at school sucked. The girl he now hung out with sucked. And now men sucked. It was hardly a surprise.

"Yeah," I said, feeling nauseated from my initiation into alcohol as I lay down on the carpet and pressed my cheek into the crimps of the shag. It felt nice against my face. I wished I had shag carpeting in my bedroom.

"Get off the floor," Jessica said, prodding me softly with her foot. "My mom'll know we've been drinking if we're lying all over the floor. Not that it matters: they went to a party, so my dad'll be hammered too." She paused, then concluded: "My dad sucks."

We heard their car pull into the driveway and we climbed into bed. The front door opened and closed, her parents clomped up the stairs, and a few terse words passed between them as they walked down the hallway towards Jessica's bedroom. Something about ". . . so don't deny it, Jack, I'm not blind . . ." and ". . . you don't know what the hell you're talking about . . ." Then Jessica's bedroom door opened.

Silence.

Jessica and I made sure our eyes were closed. Put on innocent, sleeping-young-girl expressions.

When her parents had closed the door and gone into their own bedroom, Jessica leaned over to me and whispered, "So your father's a faggot, big whoop. At least he's not a lying, cheating, son-of-a-bitch, drunken asshole."

My laughter came out as a giant snort, something that sent us both into pillow-muffled hysterics.

"So quit yer belly-achin'," she said, elbowing me under the covers. "Your life's a bed of fucking roses."

I laughed half-heartedly. Then a thought came to me. "Pansies, actually," I whispered, and we both nearly fell off the bed stifling our giggles.

Gradually, the syrup of drunken exhaustion poured over us and I heard Jessica fall asleep, her throat rustling with the faintest of snores. I couldn't sleep, the combination of nausea and the hugeness of our small lives making me feel that I was falling through space. The bed seemed to be moving, winding and twisting through the darkness. I blinked away soundless tears, the black night a thick ink against my eyes.

"I know where we are," I whispered. "We're lost."

FEBRUARY 5, 1981

WE INTERRUPT THIS PROGRAM TO BRING YOU AN
IMPORTANT ANNOUNCEMENT:

Toronto Metropolitan Police have raided four homosexual bathhouses and have arrested approximately 300
men. This is the largest mass arrest in Canada since
Prime Minister Trudeau invoked the War Measures Act
during the October Crisis of 1970, when 465 individuals were arrested and detained after the kidnappings
of two government officials.

In a series of coordinated raids code-named Operation
Soap, more than 150 Toronto police stormed four of the city's
gay bathhouses. A total of 286 men were charged with being
"found-ins" at a bawdy house, a term (with an admittedly quaint
colonial ring to it) that means brothel, essentially, or a place
where "lewd or indecent acts" take place. The employees and
owners of the bawdy houses (also an admittedly fun homonym,
for they were certainly all about *bodies*) were also detained.

The police inflicted in excess of $50,000 in damages on
the bathhouses, some of it with sledgehammers and crowbars,
and everyone on the premises was arrested, all for suspicion
of conduct that was, since the Criminal Law Amendment Act,
legal between two consenting adults in private.*

• • •

---

* This *Toronto Star* article describes the events of "Operation Soap." http://www.
thestar.com/news/gta/article/933821--thirty-years-after-the-bathhouse-raids

Despite the removal of homosexuality from the Criminal Code more than a decade earlier, in 1981 being out of the closet was still a major risk, even in Toronto. It was still legal to discriminate on the basis of sexual orientation, and being a fag could mean losing your job without recourse, risking the love of family and friends, being ostracized, being beaten up in the street (and having, let's see, the police to protect you). This was long before gay characters were written into television shows, and before talk-show hosts, athletes and celebrities began coming out publicly. Such things were still unimaginable. And these were the earliest days of a gay political presence in the city of Toronto, with its first unabashedly gay-positive and openly gay politicians.

John Sewell was mayor of Toronto at the time of the bath raids. Two years earlier, he had spoken in support of the gay newspaper *Body Politic*, as well as for the proposed amendment to the Ontario Human Rights Code that would protect gay and lesbian people from discrimination on the basis of sexual orientation. Mayor Sewell admitted later that he was surprised by the vociferous criticism and opposition he faced for taking such a stance; he hadn't counted on people actually defending discrimination.

In the 1980 Toronto municipal elections, an openly gay politician by the name of George Hislop ran for alderman. Mayor Sewell endorsed his campaign. Hislop was an amiable, down-to-earth guy in his fifties who wore business suits and had investments in a number of gay establishments. He helped found the Community Homophile Association of Toronto in 1970 and organize the first gay rights demonstrations on Parliament Hill in 1971. Hislop had been on the city Planning Commission, was well liked and well respected, and was famously wonderful with the press. His chances of being elected were good.

During the last few weeks of Hislop's campaign, however, pamphlets began circulating in his riding. One such pamphlet, published by the League Against Homosexuals, announced that "Queers Do Not Produce: They Seduce," and posed a number of questions for people to ponder:

QUESTIONS FOR TODAY'S PARENTS AND FUTURE PARENTS:
DO YOU WANT YOUR CHILDREN TAUGHT BY QUEERS?
DO YOU WISH TO HAVE YOUR CHILD TURN INTO A QUEER?
DO YOU WISH TO KILL OUR FUTURE?
DOES OUR SOCIETY NEED QUEERS?
WHO SUPPORTS QUEERS?
WHO NEEDS THE SUPPORT OF QUEERS?

Lest there be any uncertainty as to the appropriate response, the pamphlet went on:

Here Are The Answers To These Questions:
Any sane, rational, healthy society does not need queers for
  anything.

Hislop's campaign went well, although the vote count was not as high as his organizers had predicted and not quite high enough to win the election. Sewell was defeated in his bid for re-election as mayor, and many blamed his association with Hislop for his defeat.

Still, the campaign was a clear indication that a gay and lesbian political presence was developing, that issues of discrimination, status and rights would need to be addressed, and that the face of Toronto's political and cultural scene was changing.

Just one month before the bathhouse raids, in the January 1981 issue of the Toronto Metropolitan Police magazine *News & Views*, the "Best Cartoon of the Year" depicted a policeman sweeping up a street while holding a man labelled "Sewell" by the neck; in a nearby garbage can was a man labelled "Hislop." The caption read: *Just doing a bit of cleaning up.*

A month later, the police launched Operation Soap.

Once the police had forcibly opened or kicked in all doors in the bathhouses (one of which was partly owned by Hislop), the found-ins were lined up naked in the shower room and forced to submit to rectal examinations. When the first man was told to bend over and he paused in disbelief, an officer ordered him to submit, adding: "Don't tell me you haven't done that before." The other men waited, some for more than an hour, with their arms over their heads. At one point, one of the police officers shouted, "I wish these pipes were hooked up to gas so I could annihilate you all!"*

---

* From *Track Two*, a 1982 documentary by director Harry Sutherland about the 1981 Toronto bathhouse raids and riots and the events that precipitated them.

The scene had particularly painful resonance for John Burt, a found-in of European-Jewish descent, who had grown up understanding on some level what his parents had gone through in the concentration camps, but who felt, as he stood naked in that shower room—humiliated, loathed, vulnerable—a horrifying new understanding of his parents' experience.*

The police compiled an enormous amount of information from most of the found-ins, including place of employment, superior's name and phone number, and, in the case of married men, their wife's name and phone number. In the past, police had been known to make "concerned citizen" calls to employers in cases where homosexuals were charged (though of course it had never been deemed necessary to report to the employers or wives of the found-ins of *heterosexual* brothels), so those involved could only presume a round of "I know something that you don't know" calls would be going out shortly.

As news of the raids began to spread, people responded with disbelief, their numbness quickly giving way to outrage, their years of pent-up frustration and humiliation fuelling the shared conviction that a response, a demonstration, was imperative. The day following the arrests, a march was organized to protest police brutality. More than three thousand people, my father among them, flooded Yonge Street, Toronto's main thoroughfare, chanting, "Stop the cops!" and "No more raids!"

The police hadn't anticipated such a reaction—no one had—and they were unprepared. The crowds stopped traffic completely, marching and chanting all the way to the Metro

---

* From *Track Two* documentary.

Police's 52 Division, where the found-ins had been charged and released the previous night and where most of the police force now stood, surrounding the building. The crowd voiced its fury—"Fuck you, 52! Gay rights now!"—and to the barricade of guarding officers, the marchers issued a massive Nazi salute. From there, they headed up to the Provincial Legislature, where they beat at the doors until violence broke out between police and protesters and the march's organizers urged the crowd to disperse.

The police could have no idea how helpful Operation Soap would be to the gay and lesbian community, for the furious, frustrated footsteps of those protesters gathered momentum and resulted in the first great strides for gay and lesbian rights in Ontario. There had been smaller raids and marches in other cities and gay rights groups were active across the country. But it was on that cold February night of the Toronto bath-raid protest that the city's gay community emerged from the shadows and unashamedly, in great numbers, came out into the street.

When author Margaret Atwood heard about the bath raids, her response was, "What have the police got against cleanliness?" One month after the raids, she spoke at a Gay Freedom Rally in support of the found-ins. "It always made me want to throw up when I would see big kids beating up little kids on the playground. And I always wondered why they did that. And then I realized, it's because they can. Or at least, they think they can." The crowd cheered and whistled. "But I don't see why anybody, in a society that calls itself a democracy, should have to suffer from institutionalized contempt."* The gay community agreed, although there was no such thing as a "gay community" back then—not really. There were gay groups, collectives and political organizations working behind the scenes, but nothing close to the solidarity and sense of shared identity that began to emerge the night the police gave everyone a common cause to gather around.

Just as the 1969 Stonewall bathhouse raid and riots in New York had galvanized the gay and lesbian community south of the border, the 1981 Toronto bath raids marked the moment in this country that lesbians and gays stopped believing that small, quiet (Canadian-style), tiptoeing steps might be enough to secure them the respect and acceptance they deserved. It was the night that enough was finally enough. Enough of succumbing to fear. Enough buckling under to blackmail, pleading guilty and going back into the closet, as most people had done after similar raids in the past. It was the night people said, *Hang onto your hockey helmets, Canada, this country's about to get a lot more colourful.*

Or, in the words of the gay/lesbian publisher Pink Triangle Press, "The outcome that we seek is this: gay and lesbian people daring to set love free."

---

* From *Track Two* documentary.

That was Toronto. I was a hundred miles and several galaxies away in Peterborough, which was, in those days, a quiet, homogeneous town whose newspaper rose to the self-appointed task of confirming, daily, that virtually nothing of any interest or import ever occurred there.

The night of the bath raids, I was at band practice. Had been, at any rate, having developed a furious fascination for percussion shortly after I started high school, the rhythmic beating and clanging of willing objects providing me with such ineffable satisfaction that I often stayed late after practice just to whack some of the larger drums.

So while police were striking homosexuals into submission, I was probably in the music room of Crestwood High School, thwacking the cauldron head of the timpani with a hard mallet, creating a roomful of thunder cracks with my bare hands and feeling like a teenage girl version of Zeus.

I didn't learn of the raids or the protest march until much later, when Jessica Bell (who had become aloof in recent months; my mother said she looked "unhappy") casually mentioned that she had heard something about my dad from a friend down the street.

I can still feel the flames of shame that shot up from my stomach to my cheeks.

We were in Jessica's bedroom collaborating on a Harlequin-type romance story in which we would each write juicy, quasi-sexual scenes of the other being greatly desired by the hairy-chested Barry Gibb (the eldest Bee Gee). He probably sucked in real life, Jessica had told me. But in our imaginations, he could be perfect. That was the nice thing about writing. I was never very good at creating erotica, Jessica being far more worldly and knowledgeable in such matters than I. She would lie on the floor and moan, "Oh, can you just imagine what it would be like to have Barry Gibb as a *lover?*"

I couldn't. Try as I might.

But once, before she shrieked her disgust and shamed me into never uttering such a pathetic thing again in my life, I admitted that sometimes I did fantasize about having Barry Gibb as a *father.*

Hip, hairy and heterosexual. I couldn't imagine a more thrilling combination of traits to have wandering around the house.

"You're so *weird*," she said, returning to penning scenes of Barry undressing me by a poolside in Australia. (My scenes of Barry seducing her were never quite as exotic or lubricious as she hoped.)

"Oh, I forgot to tell you," she said, pen in her mouth. "Victoria Brown said that your dad's been very naughty."

I was burning within seconds. Nothing gradual about it. Just: hot.

"What," was all I could say, scarcely moving my lips. It wasn't a question at all. It was a demand. I hated Jessica in that moment. The power she held over me. *This is what happens when you tell someone about this*, I concluded, my jaw forming a hard ridge against the world. "Just tell me *what.*"

• • •

The trials for the found-ins had taken more than a year to complete (total taxpayer bill for the raids: more than $250,000) with the vast majority pleading not-guilty and winning their cases. One of the techniques of the gay rights organizers fighting the cases was to fill the courtroom with "decoys" to confuse the police, who had to identify, from among a roomful of men, those they had arrested during the raids. The decoys were gay men who resembled the accused. One of them was my dad.

One afternoon, as my father and his moustachioed friends were quack-quack-quacking around the courtroom trying to get the police to shoot confused glances in their direction, the judge arrived. *All rise.* My dad did. But he nearly sat down again when he saw the black-robed, bespectacled man presiding: Judge Brown, his former neighbour from lovely, leafy, suburban Merino Road.

Everyone having been sworn to an oath of privacy, the matter did not leave the courtroom, though somehow news of Dad's participation in the trial *and what that meant* did reach the judge's teenage children, who were kind enough not to shoot off the firecracker gossip too loudly (Jessica was told not to tell many people), and fortunately, none of them were the *nah-nah* type.

Jessica was out of rum, so once she'd divulged all the details of the gossip, we drank a pitcher of Kool-Aid with extra sugar and fell asleep with twitching eyelids and pink tongues.

We remained friends, but guardedly so. And I wasn't close to anyone after that.

How could I be.

• • •

From then on, it was difficult to shake the feeling, as I walked around the neighbourhood, that there was this teensy little gargantuan secret, and if it accidentally slipped out, well, it just might have the social effect of whacking me to my knees with a metal bar and knocking my teeth out.

And then there were the looks of pity, which might well have been worse than a metal bar to the knees. *Oh, poor you, your life's so awful*, neighbours could say with a simple glance. I had moved into the "we're fine, carry on with your lawn mowing" stage of scandalous-pansy-in-the-family living, and I didn't really relax or feel part of the neighbourhood for another few years.

Maybe ever.

In my quietest moments, I began to believe that there had to exist—far, far away—a place where none of this would matter. Where I wouldn't have to lie or pretend, where I could walk out the door, wave to neighbours, and feel like I belonged. Though I'm sure I didn't put the feeling into words at the time. It was more of a churning, a queasiness I ached to resolve. The way a seasick person longs for land. Scans the horizon for it, constantly. Dreams of it, the sensation of stillness beneath her feet. Yet the only thing visible in every direction is water. Waves everywhere.

That search for land would come to shape my adult life. It would take me to the far edges of the world, have me peering out over the edges of continents, moving through war zones and revolutions, learning languages and songs of belonging, and revelling in the sensation of being deliciously alone.

Anonymous. Suspended from the world. It was a quest that fuelled some of the richest, most fascinating periods of my life.

Who knows. If Dad had been hip, hairy and heterosexual, I might never have left Peterborough.

EMPTYING OUT

One day shortly before my fifteenth birthday, I walked into my parents' bedroom and the twin beds were gone.

"Your dad needed them for his new house," my mother said without any music in her voice at all.

And that was that.

He'd moved out for good.

I don't remember whether or not I cried.

Dad moved into an old house on a quiet residential street in a comfy neighbourhood of Toronto. He had considered buying a house closer to downtown, but a friend had warned him that his children might not feel comfortable with the neighbourhood, so my dad took the advice and chose the fixer-upper with posh-potential.

I didn't really like the place. For one thing, it smelled funny. Smelled *old*. There was gaudy wallpaper throughout that was heavy with other people's lives, and the kitchen floor sloped so severely we couldn't put a dish down on the table without it sliding off the other side. I can't remember how we ate in those days; I guess we all held our bowls. The stairs creaked excessively (still do), the bathroom was black and white with a tile floor that was always cold, and the yard was the size of two parking spaces at Kmart.

But the neighbourhood felt better than the gay ghetto: no graffiti or drag queens, lots of narrow houses with tidy little gardens, and no traffic. Toronto was still filthy, littered with cigarette butts and advertising, the subway like a rat pit. And the Chinese food Dad took us out for was all slurpy and bumpy, bowls of white spongy blobs and gooey vegetables, nothing like the chow mein and chicken balls you could get at the Crest Chinese & Canadian Restaurant at the edge of town in Peterborough.

Why live in Toronto? Especially when you still work at Trent University in Peterborough!

Why eat weird stringy food?

Why be gay?

There were so many questions I didn't have answers for and no one I felt I could ask.

Actually, I don't believe I ever thought of asking anyone anything, or that I even considered myself full of questions. I just moved into a period when my life became made up of things I did not fully understand.

Dad tried to fill our visits to Toronto with things we enjoyed, in my case ballet and chocolate. He got season tickets to the National Ballet and introduced me to things like profiteroles with extra *crème fouettée*, so quickly I began to associate the city with things less dreary and smelly.

Occasionally my brothers and I went together. Early on, when the kitchen was still slopey, Flip and I were taken to see a touring Chinese circus and we were so inspired by the superhuman feats of the troupe that we spent the rest of the evening flinging each other around Dad's house, balancing dishes on our feet and leaping from the back of the couch onto each other's shoulders. Dad came downstairs at one point— someone had fallen and was in tears, probably Flip, as I was never very good at catching—and once it was established that everyone was okay, Dad said, in a voice that was kind of froggy, as though there were tears gurgling in his throat, that he enjoyed hearing our laughter in the house.

It got a bit awkward at that point because no one wanted Dad to cry, so Flip got all cheerful and said that we sure had found the Chinese circus *stimulating*.

He knew that would cheer Dad up.

For Paul, eating, and food itself, was stimulation. He and my dad spent months scoping out the best holes-in-the-wall in Chinatown, eating dim sum, and buying bizarre Asian fruits that had prickly skins and smelled like farts. Paul went on to develop a passion for food and wine that has turned into a successful and much-loved career, which began around the age of fifteen, when he began catering the parties of our neighbours in Peterborough. Using ingredients he picked up in Chinatown and a large set of Chinese dishes my mother had given him for Christmas, Paul served multicourse meals of exquisitely prepared Chinese food to parties of astonished neighbours. It was just about the last thing anyone expected of a teenage boy on Merino Road.

I was as surprised as anyone that Paul's food was such a hit, as well as being greatly relieved. The first time he set out for the neighbours' house with all those dishes of food piled into a huge long box, I was afraid that after all that careful preparation, that endless chopping into little pieces, all that whisking and stirring of sauces, fiddly frying and drying, the neighbours might find the food as barfy as I did. But they raved and raved.

Like I said, there were so many things I did not fully understand.

Dad gutted his new (old) house bit by bit, refinishing wood floors and laying oriental carpets, replastering and painting the entire house Wedgwood blue with white trim, and filling the place with the furniture he had inherited from his parents; among other things, the twin beds my mother had said she didn't want. He hung an astonishing number of chandeliers and sconces, unpacked his collection of sketches, paintings and statues of naked men, and found places for every one of them.

My weekends in Toronto during that period were spent amid plaster dust, Chinese restaurants and Wagner operas, and gradually my brothers and I grew accustomed to the changes in our lives; not in our father, for he was largely the same (with a few added personality sequins), but in all that surrounded him. He had been coming out for about two years by the time he bought his house, so we were already used to seeing copies of *Body Politic: gay liberation journal* lying around. Many of his new friends had a way of speaking that identified them clearly as "gay" (not quite as pronounced as "Thammy" from the Gay Fathers of Toronto potluck, but thimilar). And they were suddenly not all academics but also *normal* people: postal workers, Bell Canada employees, architects, dessert chefs, lawyers, opera singers, and a journalist/prostitute who was the least pretentious well-read person I'd ever met.

While I found it strange that my dad was suddenly hanging around with postmen and prostitutes, I must have been young enough to not really care. (Incidentally, the journalist/prostitute looked and dressed like a university professor, and a few years after I met him, he became one.) Or rather, I must have been young enough still to care more about what they were like than what they did for a living. I was also young enough to continue to take cues from my dad, who didn't seem to find any of it strange at all. And I was so used to his university friends speaking excessively syllabic nonsense about things that mattered only to them that it was a relief to spend time with people who spoke real English about things that also mattered to me.

Also, these guys were *fun*. They loved to make jokes. Make light of things. Double over giggling. Groan about good chocolate. The whole thing might have been considerably harder if Dad's new circle of colourful friends hadn't been so likeable. But they were engaging and interesting, mirthful and eager to chat. I truly enjoyed hanging out with them. By the time Dad introduced me to his "boyfriend"—the postman as it turned out—I was so taken by the man's playfulness that I came away hoping only that they wouldn't split up, so that he could continue to be my friend.

Which he has done. For more than thirty years.

It never occurred to me to hate Dad for being gay, nor did the notion ever seem to dawn on my brothers. There were plenty of times when I was angry about the whole thing—deeply sad, actually, though hiding it beneath a mask of cool teenage ire—but to wag my finger at Dad's willy and get all worked up about what he was choosing to do with it never crossed my mind. Somehow, my brothers and I understood that the "sex part" had nothing to do with us. And that to be furious at him for being gay was as pointless as cursing a bat for hanging by its feet.

What I did hate was the Greyhound bus, that long sprint on the dog's back to and from Toronto, the grime and stink of it, the feel of the highway in my chest; to this day the reek of bus fumes throws me into a nauseated funk. I hated the shame my mother wore in her eyes, the way she would sit in the La-Z-Boy rocking chair in the backroom listening to old, scratchy recordings of Schubert *Lieder* and swimming in a pain for which the world had no place. I hated that it was the day of Flip's ninth birthday party that she had discovered a love letter from her husband to a man—*pin the tail on the donkey everyone!*— and that after the party she decided to go camping by herself. Two cans of tuna, a loaf of black bread, a husband in love with a man, and a life with three young children to figure out.

I hated that they fought over money. I hated it when my mother walked around looking like a top that was all bound up and busting to have her string pulled so she could spin. I hated that, especially by comparison, my dad seemed so damn happy. But more than anything else, I hated all the stories I needed to invent about my life, the dancing pink elephant in the room that I spent my adolescence trying to conceal.

I became an acutely talented liar. Could talk for hours about things that never happened, tire people with details of the illustrious job at the University of Toronto that had forced my dad to move (in truth, he still taught at Trent University and lived, during the week, in a house with some other gay profs across town). I claimed great vexation at my mother's refusal to move the family to the city, throwing in enough histrionic gestures to make my frustration believable. As my friends chewed their bland sandwiches in the cafeteria, I would regale them with tales of the dazzling and mythical metropolis of Toronto—the restaurants, the films, the concerts, the *art* (a word I learned very young to use as a weapon of superiority)— all the while conveying my sympathies that both their parents lived in poky, dull, provincial little Peterborough. Probably even shared a bed. Lamentable things.

In addition to the piano, my mother also played the oboe, a notoriously difficult reed instrument that when played badly sounds like a Canada goose with croup, but when played well creates one of the most sublime sounds on this earth. My mother's playing was on the sublime end of the scale, although she never considered herself a master of the instrument.

The oboe bears a superficial resemblance to the clarinet, but the oboe is played with a double reed stuck into a hole at the top of the instrument, rather than a single reed on the side of the mouthpiece. Oboists being a rare breed (in Peterborough, there was, let's see . . . one: my mom), she had to make her own double reeds, which she did by cutting two pieces of cane with a very sharp knife, binding them together with red thread and sticking them into a tube of cork, which fit into the top of her instrument.

Sounds simple enough, and it is relatively easy to make a reed that goes *squawk*, but making a good reed is an art in itself and for years my mother devoted herself to it. Our yellow kitchen chairs, strands of red thread forever dangling from them, were testaments to this devotion, as my mother's technique involved using the chairs as ballast while she wound the red thread around and around the cane, stacking each layer of coiled thread neatly upon the last, the chair back holding the thread tight. When she was finished, she would snip the red thread, make a firm knot and stick the reed in her mouth—*pee-peepeepeeeeeep*—to test it out. There would always be adjustments to make: chiselling with the sharp knife, shaving a bit off here or there. Sometimes, she would have to make so many cuts and shavings that the reed would be ruined. But other times, she would hover over her small grindstone, chiselling and shaving, playing a few *peep*s, chiselling again, until the *peeep* was just right. Then she would plug the reed into her oboe, play a few velvet passages, and pull the reed out with a smile of triumph. "I just made a great reed!" she would proclaim.

I swear dinner always tasted better on those nights. And lying in bed that night would be like flying through stars, the song of my mom's oboe downstairs threading constellations of light through the dark house, guiding us on our nightly migration into sleep.

It was probably the sheer relief and satisfaction that came with producing a great reed that made Mom forget to snip the rest of the red thread from the back of the yellow kitchen chairs, and over the years those chairs became hairy with dangling threads. It became sort of comforting, in that my brothers and I took to throwing our arms over the backs of the chairs and running our fingers through the threads the way some people play with their hair.

And that is what I was doing—coiling the thread around my finger, then letting it loosen and fall, over and over—the night she went out to orchestra practice the year after Dad moved out and I decided to snoop through her desk in the corner of the kitchen. Actually, I did that a lot. Sometimes the car wouldn't even get halfway down the driveway before

I popped open the metal doors (it wasn't a typical wooden desk—more of a metal cabinet with a wooden flap she could pull up to do her filing and chiselling on) and started riffling through whatever papers I could find.

It was there that I had found the divorce papers for *Wearing vs. Wearing*, those long typed pages, most of which I didn't understand, but where a single typed word, *Homosexuality*, was listed as the grounds for divorce.

I remember staring at that word for a long time, one hand running through my mother's red threads, my tears blurring the letters together, as I tried to fit my dad into that word. I knew that he was gay, that was not news, but it was a deeply sad and lonely moment still. Something condemning and denouncing about it made me just cry and cry.

Snooping was also how I learned, a few months later, that my mother was getting remarried. "Well, I assume you've heard all the bad news," she wrote in a half-finished, clearly long-overdue letter to an old friend in England, "but the good news is that I am getting married . . ."

I wound the thread so hard around my fingers that time that I nearly cut off the circulation.

Several months after my dad moved out, my mother began playing tennis with a neighbour. Mel was a friendly man with an eager smile, the kind of person who did things like bound up the stairs two at a time. Mel had lived around the corner from us for as long as I could remember, but I never really knew him (other than as "that divorced guy who lives on Roper Drive"), and the idea of my mother "dating Mel" was one of the weirdest things I could have imagined.

Mel loved sailing and adventures and pulling into our driveway in his long, fake-wood station wagon and asking my mother to "go out for cappuccino." It was the first time in as long as I could remember that my mother had a social life outside the house.

I was furious.

Terrified, actually. Convinced she was going to disappear too. To restore order to the world, I began keeping tabs on her like a probation officer. She was required to file her whereabouts with me at all times. More than once, I had her paged at a restaurant for flouting her responsibilities and staying out ten minutes later than she had promised. She was often frustrated by the choke-chain I'd looped around her life, but when I burst into tears she would soothe me, saying, "You don't have to worry" and "I'm not going to just run off."

My mother's outings didn't seem to bother either of my brothers—nothing seemed to—but I was constantly filled with anxiety. If my mother said she was going out to play tennis, I'd decide to take the dogs for a walk so that I could keep an eye on her from a neighbouring field. If she said she was going to Mel's house for dinner, I would show up at his door when I felt they should be finished eating.

Understandably it drove my mother bonkers, but she and Mel tried to be sympathetic and provide me with the assurance I needed. Until one evening about half a year into their courtship when my mother announced over dinner that she and Mel were going to Aruba.

"What's a Ruba?" Flip asked between mouthfuls of green beans.

But I knew exactly what it was. It was *running off with someone.* Goddamn them.

"When are you leaving?" I pried petulantly, as furious as I was upset.

"Tomorrow," my mother responded calmly. Her sister, Sally, would come to stay with us for the week.

"For the rest of our lives, more like it!" I yelled, and stormed up to my room.

That night, I crept into my mother's room and begged her not to go, even launching a case for why it would be a good idea to stop seeing Mel altogether. He wasn't her type. Didn't even play an instrument. Wouldn't know a concerto from a contact lens. She should stay home and play the piano more. She hardly ever did that anymore. Wasn't that a bad sign? Besides, he was a *sailor.* And you just never know what kind of a thing a person like *that* is going to do.

I didn't win my case, but I wept dramatically and made her promise me that she would come back. Although I don't know why I bothered because I didn't believe her when she did.

When she walked out the door the next day, I took a conscious snapshot of her face—her uniquely gorgeous, irreplaceable smile—convinced it would be the last time I would ever see her.

(It wouldn't have dawned on me to create such drama over one of my dad's departures. He had come and gone for so long, I never imagined I had any control over his whereabouts. And he had *always* had a social life outside the house. But if the double standard drove my mother "round the bend," she never pointed it out to me.)

As promised, she returned from the Caribbean. *They* returned. And sometime after that, she went out to orchestra practice, handmade reeds in hand, and I went snooping and found the letter. So while I was surprised by the news of an actual wedding, it didn't come wholly without warning. And considering my near-crazed reaction to her mating dance with Mel, I can understand her wanting to enjoy the exciting news with her friends for a bit before initiating what was sure to be a Heavy Conversation with me.

In the end, the conversation appears to have been so heavy it collapsed my memory, for I have no recollection of it at all. I probably cried so hard I washed all traces of the words away. Actually, I think I was angry. Yes, I vaguely remember storming off the back porch and slamming the sliding door shut, hoping its large glass would shatter. Oh, and I recall one of our sweet little Bichon Frisés nearly getting squashed in the slam.

In any case, they got married, and suddenly I had a stepfather named Melville.

I didn't like him. For one, he had stolen my mother. For another, I found him exceedingly heterosexual: he belonged to the Kiwanis Club, was an engineer, a *sailor*, and he viewed the kitchen as a woman's domain. And every night when he came home from work, he would put his briefcase on the kitchen table, reach up to the top cupboard and pour himself a scotch.

Sometimes another.

And another.

"I heard my mom telling Mrs. Smithey she's so relieved your mom got remarried," Jessica told me as we sat on the floor of her room listening to her latest passion: the music of KISS. "Yeah," Jessica said, putting on a nasal imitation of her mother's voice. *"Now those kids can finally get back to having a normal life."*

MARRIAGE AND MUSHROOMS

Our first Christmas as a new family was kaleidoscopic. The wedding had taken place a few months earlier and all seven children—my brothers (ages twelve and sixteen), me (fifteen), and Mel's four kids (between seventeen and twenty-three)—were still adjusting to the new configuration of our lives. All of us, I believe, with some difficulty.

Mel's kids had flown in from Halifax (where their mother lived) for a week starting on Christmas Eve. The first afternoon was a series of awkward introductions and silences, the evening a painful attempt by the newlyweds to highlight how much we all had in common. Apart from choruses of throat-clearing, the dominant sound at the dinner table was the scraping of cutlery against plates. Once the dinner was adjourned, I slipped out the back door, punched through the thigh-deep snow of the neighbourhood's backyards and crawled into Jessica's basement. I found her listening to Pink Floyd and slurping hootched-up Coke, and we spent the next few hours trading ongoing tragedies.

The next morning came far too early, my hungover head feeling like a gravel driveway that someone had spent the night shovelling. I came downstairs to an intimate Christmas morning of total strangers and the CBC. Passing over the plate of store-bought croissants on the counter, I put a piece of bread in the toaster and accepted a cup of spiced tea that my stepbrothers had prepared. My new stepsister was quiet but pleasant, helping my mother get everyone accommodated.

They were friendly, my stepbrothers, funny and charming, and, it bears mentioning (because I was a teenage girl whose interest in erotica was steadily growing), they were also drop-dead cute. I hadn't noticed the previous night, so focused had I been on my new-family anxiety. But over the course of break-fast, despite my bedraggled, dry-mouthed state, I found myself warming up to them. The older one in particular. No, the middle one. The deep brown saucers of his eyes. As I crunched dry toast and glugged cup after cup of sweet spiced tea, I found myself beginning to enjoy the allure of my new family.

After everyone had eaten, we went into the living room for the traditional opening of presents. And that was where it all began to twist. Well, not twist exactly, more like undulate, with gal-loping shapes and colours. And presents, so many presents. So many presents that I felt they were filling the room, crawling along the carpet and gathering around my shoulders. I got up and went into the hallway. Scrunched my eyes. Stared at the ceiling, the floor. My stepbrother appeared, the middle one with the dreamy eyes, put a hand on my shoulder and asked if I was all right. Yeah, I said, blinking excessively. I moved to touch his face only to discover that my fingers were dancing green lights. Five glowing threads attached to my wrist. I played with them for a while, dangling and dancing them in front of my face, until he guided me back into the living room, where Mel was in the process of opening a small oblong box from his eldest son.

"Look at this tie! Oh, Anne! *Look* at this tie!" he repeated, shaking his head in amazement.

My mother paid no attention, focused as she was on hooking a pair of slippers over her ears and kicking her legs side to side like a showgirl. Mel stared at her bewildered (as did we all), but said nothing. Instead, he returned the lid to the gift box, stared around the room with an entranced expression, and then, returning his gaze to the box, opened it again. "Look at this tie!" he exclaimed, as though seeing it for the first time. "Oh, Anne, look at this tie!"

He repeated the whole exercise so many times, it seemed the room had fallen into some kind of time-warped loop.

"Oh, Anne, *look* at this tie!" he gasped for the nth time, one hand pressed to his forehead.

But she did not, of course, because of all the Folies Bergère ear-slipper dancing.

It was the greatest lunacy I had ever beheld.

My stepbrothers, all three of them, were a heap of entangled limbs in one corner of the room, laughing so hard their eyes streamed with tears. My own brothers sat side by side on the green-striped loveseat, their heads volleying back and forth as though watching a tennis match, their bottom lips flaccid, cheeks long.

Eventually, although it was the middle of the day, people started going to bed. Or rather, our parents went to bed while some of the kids napped on the sofa and others stayed up drinking Irish coffee at the suggestion of the good-looking middle stepbrother. I took a catnap in an armchair and woke up ravenous. It was two in the afternoon but I felt like I hadn't eaten in days. My brothers and stepsiblings were all in the kitchen, scavenging through the fridge and cupboards like army ants, gnawing croissant ends, eating jam by the spoonful, and slathering (still-frozen) french fries with peanut butter. There was a raw hot dog stuck in the top of the ketchup bottle. "I tried to dip it," my eldest stepbrother explained, and we all found this so monstrously funny that I thought I was going to pee my pants.

Then we began to play poker, heaps of white-red-blue plastic chips being piled on flushes, bluffs and avalanches of laughter, until my mother stumbled in mid-afternoon, her hair all pushed up on one side as though she'd been trying to curl it with a frying pan, asking what we should do about the turkey.

As I recall, Christmas dinner didn't happen that year until about midnight, by which time my new siblings and I had all dyed our hair pink. There were none of the tedious *scrape-scrape* silences of the previous evening, and moments after the last of the pumpkin pie had been shovelled into our eager mouths, we were outside collecting boulder-sized snowballs from the ends of people's driveways, heaving them at one another and roaring like lions up and down the length of our quiet, plowed, festively lit street.

Eventually, we learned that the spiced tea my stepbrothers made for us that memorable Christmas morning had been mulled not just with cloves, cinnamon, star anise, but also with magic mushrooms, that festive hallucinogen guaranteed to liven up any staid affair.

A few days after the mushroom Christmas, Paul, Flip and I travelled to Toronto to celebrate the holidays with our dad and his (now serious) boyfriend, Lance. There were a few wrapped gifts for each of the kids under the tree (Dad and Lance having exchanged gifts on Christmas morning), and a few from us to them. Dad gave me a deep-burgundy angora turtleneck sweater, and he and I took turns rubbing our cheeks against the wool and groaning at its softness. Lance gave me a book on the Kirov Ballet, which I found quite wonderful, and I don't remember what Paul and Flip got and probably didn't notice even then.

With choral music playing in the background, we ate dinner: turkey, roasted parsnips, mashed potatoes, Brussels sprouts, and homemade cranberry sauce. And after dinner Dad set up the slide projector and we all guided Lance through our early family adventures, an experience that must have been about as pleasant as having children decide to give you a root canal, but Lance was a good sport about it. And then we all wished each other a merry late Christmas and went to bed.

It was pretty, um, *normal*. One might even say "traditional."

Except for the thing about my dad and Lance having the same anatomy.

"So, what have you been up to tonight?"

(The pickup line that changed my father's life.)

"Well, I just went to see a performance of *Oklahoma!* at the Royal Alex."

(The sing-songy reply that would come to change our lives as well.)

The setting: Buddy's. One of Toronto's gay bars.

The date: April 3, 1981.

The protagonists: my dad (Mr. Pickup) and Lance.

Hailing from Alberta farming stock, Lance spent much of his childhood in the town of Kelowna in the interior of British Columbia. He was one of four children, and his three sisters love to claim that Lance once pushed his younger sister out of the family car as they were driving down the highway. According to Lance, they were driving along with the windows down, happily admiring the summer day around them, when little Marjory began fiddling with the car door. The next quick, silent, pre-seat-belt-era moments included the back door opening, Marjory toppling out, the back door closing.

Just as he took a breath and leaned forward to report the tumble to his parents, Lance's mother turned around. "Where's Marjory?" she cried. "Lance! Did you push your sister out of the car?" Then, to her husband: "Lance pushed Marjory out of the car!"

Lance remembers only sputtering.

"So what happened to Marjory?" I asked, wide-eyed.

"Well, nothing!" Lance said, his voice as tuneful as a slide whistle. "She must have just kind of . . . *rolled*!"

How to describe Lance . . .

Well, assuming for a moment that there is such a thing as a spectrum of sexuality upon which most of us find ourselves weighing in at the heterosexual side of things, lesbians and gay men would be comfortable on the homosexual end, and still others would place themselves somewhere in the middle or on another spectrum altogether. Lance, were he to climb upon such a scale, would rush posthaste to the homosexual end, curl his toes over the spectrum's very edge, and lean out. Then he would turn back to the rest of the homos gathered at his end and ask which one of them was planning to serve hors d'oeuvres.

Although I don't believe he ever came out to either of his parents, Lance knew from an early age what his leanings were and they were never once, not for an instant, in the direction of a girl. After studying at the University of British Columbia in Vancouver, he was relieved to meet up at last with other gay men. Playful to the nines, the friends liked to refer to each other using campy drag names, so in due course Lance became Mona del Kelowna.

Although he was a truck driver for the post office when I met him, Lance eventually went back to school and completed a degree in one of his many abiding passions, urban planning. Name any city in the industrialized world and Lance can give you a historical architectural tour so comprehensive you will feel almost obliged to give him a tip. And that's just architecture. Ask about music, literature, politics, theatre. I know of no one more well read and well versed on as many subjects as Lance, nor as gut-splittingly funny or astutely entertaining.

Nor as bossy or opinionated—and he will take that statement as a compliment.

"I hope you're going to a lot of trouble," he has been known to warble feebly from the living room when my father is preparing dinner in the kitchen. And his terse response to learning of my plans to travel to Ecuador after university was delivered with a roll of the eyes: "Why would you want to go *there*? They don't even have an opera house!"

That said, during all the years that I travelled from one country-without-opera-house to another, whenever I found myself resurfacing from a remote adventure and stumbling to the *poste restante* address I had sent to people as my next destination, I could always count on at least one (and often several) long, newsy and hilarious letters from Lance.

While he has never felt like a parent to me, Lance does feel like family, and is. His relationship with my father has always been loyal, lively and loving (if bossy), fascinating (if fastidious), endlessly social, and laced with travel, food, (too much) opera, inspiration, stories and laughter.

I cannot think of anything objectionable about their relationship. It was always difficult to understand why anyone would.

While my dad had managed to come out of the closet completely, in my own life I kept him firmly inside it, still hiding
his life from everyone except Jessica Bell. Which meant that I
began leading a version of the double life from which my dad
had finally liberated himself.

In Toronto, I would dress up and play the princess, attending ballets and dinner parties with Dad and Lance's friends,
whom I adored. It was all still a bit *strange*, I suppose, but once
my internal compass settled around Dad's new orientation, my
Toronto weekends took on a relaxed quality: pleasantly predictable and predictably pleasant. I even began to like "real"
Chinese food.

At the end of the weekend, I would hang that life in a
closet on Walmsley Boulevard and take the Greyhound bus
back to Peterborough, already scripting what I would say to
my friends when we compared *whad'ya do this weekend?* stories.

What actually happened:

Friday night: Lance and I went to the ballet with free
tickets that he got because *his* ex-boyfriend is in the company.
Saturday: went silk-shirt shopping with my dad, then to the
new gay cult film, *My Beautiful Laundrette*, after which I adjusted
to an odd father–daughter moment that found us agreeing on
who was cuter. Sunday: enjoyed a picnic with some friends
from Gay Fathers.

What I would say happened:

My dad's neighbour (invent plausible name: maybe Jeremy

Lipton) had tickets to the ballet that he couldn't use, so he suggested that his son (named . . . um . . . Alastair: he's *gorgeous* and goes to Upper Canada College) take me. Afterwards, the two of us went to a little French bistro (the likes of which you can *only* find in Toronto), where we shared champagne and a chocolate mousse, and the next day the doorbell rang and there was a box tied with a ribbon sitting on my dad's front step. In it was *this silk shirt.* (Gasps all around.) Et cetera.

I don't know how my brothers coped, as we spoke very little in those days, Paul having entered into that Neanderthal phase of male adolescence—uh? yuh. wuh? uh-huh—and Flip being so blasé about the whole thing that he saw no point in doing anything so boring as talking about our lives when we could be flinging ourselves around the room à la Chinese circus.

While Paul and I had both needed to have The Conversation with one of our parents, Flip was young enough—nine years old when Dad came out—that he simply grew up with things as they were. Santa Claus parade in December, Gay Pride Day parade in July, summer camp with other boys, canoe trips with men and boys. Of the three of us, he probably had the easiest time of it, because there was never any "it"; there was just life as it was, changing and evolving. As life does.

I don't believe that either of my brothers felt the need to brazenly fabricate to the extent that I did. No doubt they chose the simpler, more honourable route of going about their lives normally and just not mentioning the bit about my dad and Lance being a couple. I have no idea why I didn't choose that route for myself; the lying was as exhausting as it was distracting. But my father once said that I always enjoyed telling stories with a lot of "Byzantine ornamentation" and that his mother was very much the same. So perhaps it was partly my personality, partly the fact that I was a girl (boys, even when they grow up, don't seem to feel the same need to self-expose), and partly that I had inherited the Byzantine ornamentation gene. Whatever the cause, I was constantly creating for myself a life that wasn't actually happening.

Call it fictional freedom.

BORDERS AND CREAM PUFFS

Children of parents who live separately have no trouble understanding what a border crossing is between countries, for we
contain a similar cleft within ourselves: between mother and
father, varying styles of homes and comforts, rules and expectations. It's not a bad thing, and it might even make us more
adaptable, more understanding of diversity and respectful of
different ways of being in the world. Those of us who trundle
between parents are seasoned travellers before we ever leave
our home country.

In some cases, the border is virtually non-existent, a sort
of Switzerland-to-Austria arrangement that sees mild differences in culture and codes of law, a shared language and respectful communication (peppered with private eye-rolling). In
other families, the border is more Middle Eastern in feeling,
rife with suspicions (real or imagined), accusations (real or imagined), and so thoroughly saturated with hatred and mistrust
that the children's internal landscape grows up around emotional landmines and barbed fences that they might well spend
their adult lives untangling or detonating.

In our case, the border was definitely more peaceful in
nature, a variation on the modern English–French relationship
perhaps, with the latter seeing the former as a nation of tire-
some pricks who would one day, with any luck, piss off and get
over themselves, and the former in the middle of a grand tea
party with puffy little scones and sandwiches with the crusts
cut off, wondering what all the fuss was about.

Well, that's unfair to both of them; but that was the basic picture.

While my father dreamed of friendship with my mother, Christmases together and general bonhomie, relations soured over the course of the drawn-out divorce, and by the time my mother and Mel were married (a few months after the divorce was official), a clear border had been established and my brothers and I travelled the concrete equivalent of the English Channel between our parents.

Contrary to the Sturm und Drang I enacted before Mel's establishment in our lives, there was no great kabang when Lance moved in, as there might have been if we had lived with my dad full-time or been used to his constant attention. When they did live together, Dad and Lance continued to enjoy separate lives and social circles, and while some overlapped, there weren't the sort of spousal arrangements and expectations I saw in the rest of the world. To this day, Lance has never had a particular role or label in our lives (although I teasingly call him my fairy stepmother), and in the early days he was just friendly and endlessly humorous, never tried to be a parental figure (clever, because two of us were teenagers), and he effortlessly gave our relationship with our father a lot of space.

Something none of us really noticed, but all appreciated.

Within his and my father's relationship, there were no set roles or precedents. And the freedom of that registered with me even in my desperate-to-be-normal teenage state. Like many gay couples, Dad and Lance had separate bedrooms, and that felt so instinctively healthy to me that I vowed to carry the practice into my own adult life. That they were attracted to each other and had a sex life was the least interesting thing about their relationship, as far as I was concerned, and while the idea of it did undoubtedly gross me out, it did so no more than contemplating the same details of my mother and Mel's bedroom life.

The thing about having a gay parent is that so long as the rest of society can get over it, the "gay" part isn't nearly as important as the "parent" part; in fact, it's incidental. Constancy of love, truthfulness of heart, and joyfulness of life count infinitely more than who is doing what with which gender in the bedroom. Being in the presence of love is being in the presence of love; ultimately, it is the only thing that truly matters.

I must admit to growing weary of certain things, however. The perennial Playgirl calendar in the bathroom. Being taken to any film, play or reading that so much as hinted at having gay content. The opera that greeted me the moment I opened the door to the house on Friday afternoons; the opera that blared during the hours it would take my dad to make dinner, gourmet meals being the order of the day, daily; the opera that blared Saturday mornings, and all the rest of the weekend.

But somewhere around the age of sixteen, at one of Dad and Lance's innumerable all-male-but-me dinner parties, I had an epiphany.

I was helping whip the cream that Dad would spoon into his homemade pastry puffs, which were baking in the oven.

A couple of guys were in the dining room with Lance singing a very dramatic version of "How About You?" and out on the back patio, an extremely cute Asian guy was doing mock ballet moves to an appreciative, hooting audience of three or four. My dad's friend Scott, meanwhile, was melting chocolate on the stove and regaling us with an animated description of a family reunion complete with impersonations of eccentric aunts that had us literally doubled over and choking with laughter, and in that ridiculous, *très gai* moment, I wanted to step onto the nearest skyscraper and scream to the whole world that I would far rather hang out with these crazy fairies than most of the boring oafs my friends had for dads.

Eighteen years separated my dad from his brother, an age difference so great that it almost kept them from being siblings,
Dick having already moved out of the family home by the time
my dad was old enough to play. Dick married Millie, a petite
woman who reminded me of a paper doll whose perfectly
matched clothing seemed to fold to her curveless frame like
cut-out attachments. Her hair was short and *done*. No wisps
or strands out of place. Likewise for their house, which was
so clean and orderly it looked as though no one actually lived
there. Aunt Millie was famous for not being able to sleep with
anything dirty in the house, so nightly loads of laundry were
compulsory, as was washing, drying and putting away every
dish used that day. No late-night scoop of ice cream and spoon
tossed nonchalantly into the sink in *that* household.

One of the few times we visited them in their home in
London, Ontario, our car had not even fully backed down the
driveway before Aunt Millie began sweeping up some dirt that
Paul, Flip and I had tracked onto their walkway while playing
after lunch.

"Millie's always liked a tidy house," my dad explained,
waving at Millie one last time before we pulled away. Millie
raised one hand from the broom just long enough to wave back,
then continued sweeping. "I remember one Sunday dinner
shortly after Dick and Millie were married. Our whole family
was around the table and out of the blue my grandmother, who
was rather outspoken, told everyone, 'When we were children,

we used to ask, *Which would you rather have: a messy, happy wife or a tidy, grumpy one?*'"

"Did everyone vote for the happy, messy one?" Paul asked.

My mother raised her fists and cheered. "Yes, here's to the happy, messy one!"

"Now, now," Dad said, a bit reproachfully. "Millie's very sweet. I don't think anyone voted for anyone, but I remember my mother scolding Grandmother afterwards: 'Mother, just because you're eighty-five doesn't mean you can just say anything you please!' But Grandmother just ignored her."

Uncle Dick was an obstetrician, and in one of the most coveted (but perhaps apocryphal) chapters of family lore, he and Millie were having dinner at the local golf club—pardon me, The Club—when the woman seated opposite Millie asked if Dick had always adored babies and was that why he chose to specialize in the happy field of obstetrics.

"No," Millie answered. "Dick had planned to go into dentistry, but he decided he didn't want to spend all of his days sticking his fingers into other people's mouths." She dabbed the sides of her mouth with her napkin. "So he went into obstetrics."

My dad and Dick had one sister, Dot, and she was as different from Millie as a woman could get without becoming another species. Dot was bold. Opinionated. Had humour up the wazoo. Laughed so hard her shoulders actually moved up and down. A lot. Believed that life was meant to be enjoyed. Had a sign in her kitchen that proudly proclaimed: *A clean house is the sign of a wasted life.* And an invisible one that read: *Here's the kitchen. I'll be in the den.*

Dot married young and had three children spaced fairly evenly apart followed by a fourth ten years later. Her youngest child, Amy, was Paul's age, so we were playmate-cousins from the get-go. Dot's husband, Oscar, was in the insurance business, but mostly I remember him lying in the den watching television, singing strange wandering tunes as he walked around the house, or calling Dot from a long distance off. "Daaaaaaawwwt?" he'd bellow from the kitchen, even if she was upstairs. "Why would you buy these carrots? They're so small, they only last for one bite. Now, why in the world would you go and buy carrots that are so small they aren't even real carrots? The next time you go out, just get real carrots . . ."

Dot rarely replied. If she was in the den, she'd grab the TV remote and turn up the volume, and if she was on the front porch, she would lift her newspaper so that it covered her face, as if the paper might shield some of the noise.

After fifty years of marriage, Oscar developed dementia and lived his last years in a nursing home. At eighty-nine, Dot still lives at home.

The last time I went to visit Aunt Dot, I let myself in the front door (everyone lets themselves in the front door at her place) and was greeted by the words, "Oh, hi, you made it! I'm in the middle of watching a golf game, so get yourself a beer from the fridge."

In fairness, she did turn off the television a few minutes after I sat down, and we chatted and laughed until dinnertime, at which point she announced, "It's Thursday, so I'm going to have pork and beans from a can, but you probably won't like that, so why don't we each just do our own damn thing?"

We did. And not long after the dinner hour, people began letting themselves in the front door and settling on the front porch with a beer from Dot's fridge: a neighbour freshly back from a sailing trip and full of stories, a friend from across town who needed to get out of the house because her grandchildren were visiting and pushing her patience to the brink, one of Dot's sons-in-law who was driving home and saw people on the porch so thought he'd join us, and a friend of one of Dot's daughters, a woman my age who confessed that since her divorce, she came over all the time, because when she was around Aunt Dot she always felt good.

When my father's brother, Dick, first learned that my dad was exploring "a homosexual lifestyle," Dick consulted with a psychiatrist, who told him, "Once that happens, there's nothing that can be done to change them." Dick decided the doctor was wrong, arranging for my dad to have ten sessions with a different psychiatrist. To placate his brother, Dad agreed.

The psychiatrist walked my dad back through his life in the expected fashion: relationship with father, a hard-working man who had started out a lumberjack and ended up a judge and who died when my dad was ten (all sorts of potential paternal issues here); relationship with mother, an early feminist (more potential issues here) who died shortly after my dad and mom were married; relationship with wife, good, although my dad had found himself attracted to men throughout his life, but hadn't acted on the desire until age forty. He had begun to explore the gay scene in Toronto and felt a welcome certainty about his sexual orientation, but he felt very conflicted about his marriage and family responsibilities. And so on.

At the end of the tenth appointment, the psychiatrist told my dad that if there was anything else he wanted to "work on," they could continue their sessions.

"I'd like to work on getting a man," Dad answered. "But I don't suppose you can help me with that."

The psychiatrist agreed that he could not.

From that point on, Dick chose not to have any further contact with his brother.

It was not an uncommon reaction, particularly in those days, and I believe my dad expected that after some time Dick might change his mind. He did. But only on his deathbed, twenty years later, when he requested that my dad visit him in the hospital. Dick gave Dad some of their father's papers, the two brothers had a few bedside conversations, and then Dick died.

Millie and her children invited my dad to speak at the funeral, which he did, talking about Dick in glowing terms and saying only that at one point the two of them had had different views about life and how it should be lived, but that in the end they had managed to put differences aside. "Our parents would have been proud."

Dick's children had never broken contact with my dad in the first place and they continue to be in touch. Millie kept up with my dad until she died.

While my dad had never been close to Dick, he and his sister Dot were two peas in a pod. Or no, that's too sedate. They were more like two balls in a racketball court. My dad's shoulders don't shake up and down when he laughs, but his laughter is equally expressive in its own way (and extremely embarrassing, when you are a teenager and are taken to see a comic play, and people in the rows ahead of you turn around to see who is going *whoo-hoo-hoo!*). So when Dad and Dot were laughing together, the hullabaloo was enough to drive away birds perched in nearby trees. Before Dad came out, we would spend time with Dot and her family every summer in the beautiful lakeside town of Goderich, Ontario, and she and Dad always made merry, whether it was at the beach or around the dinner table, in the kitchen or on the front porch. The two of them told stories and laughed until it was late and they were exhausted and there was nothing else to do but go to bed.

The day my dad tried to tell Dot he was gay and would be leaving his wife and children, Dot was upset, confused and, above all, horrified. *How could he do such a thing to his family?* A few weeks later, when my mother broke the news to my dad that Dot had decided "not to see him anymore," he was so devastated he went into the living room and cried inconsolably. He told me later that he wasn't sure he would ever be able to stop. While she had always had a stubborn streak, Dot and my dad had always been very close, so he hoped that with time she would come to understand and accept him.

About a year after their last communication, I was in a school production of *West Side Story*, that *Romeo and Juliet*–inspired musical set amid gritty New York gangs. The set designer-choreographer was a brilliant artist who should have been working somewhere far loftier than a west end Peterborough high school (but thankfully, for our sake, was not), the director was visionary and daring, and the conductor was exacting. It was actually a pretty good show.

I played Anybodys, a tomboy who joins the boys' gang, and the part suited me perfectly, as most of that year I walked around wanting to kick the walls in, but smiling and being nice to everyone instead.

While the rest of my school day was brain-bloating, a series of exercises that flexed my cerebral left hemisphere and asphyxiated the rest of me, the world of *West Side Story* was expansive and invigorating. I adored the community and camaraderie of our rehearsals, the challenges of rhythm and choreography, the natural elation born of the act of creation. There on the set of *West Side Story* I took my only deep breaths of that year.

We put on about seven performances and somehow—by agonizing coincidence or fate—my parents happened to come on the same night. Just to increase the Agony Index, my dad brought Lance, and my mom and Mel brought Dot, who was visiting them for the weekend, my mom and Dot having made the decision to remain friends despite the divorce.

The irony of the feuding families attending a performance about, of all things, feuding families, did not escape my dad, who apparently tried, during the intermission, to approach his sister and point this out to her. Perhaps to call it out, plead with her. Perhaps turn over a few chairs in pursuit of her as she walked away. I was back in the dressing rooms, so I didn't witness what happened, but word travelled fast that there was a shocking scene playing itself out in the auditorium, and I've never wished myself dead more fervently than I did that night between Act One and Act Two.

I'm never going to get over this, my mother thought to herself as the real-life drama played out before her. I don't know what Dot said to herself, if anything. She never spoke of the incident to anyone. And in the thirty-plus years that have followed, she has never spoken to my father again.

For most of the rest of high school, I would eat a light breakfast and, inasmuch as I could help it, nothing for the rest of the day except eight cans of Diet Coke. Then I would go jogging. I drew heavy black lines around my eyes with the idea, I believe, that no one would be able to see me underneath them. I managed to do well in most classes except Biology and English, both of which required me to pull apart a once-living creature limb by limb, labelling each piece as it was separated and pinned: heart, lungs, liver; plot, character, setting. The compulsory dissection brought me no closer to understanding frogs than it did books, and I ended up alienated from two previous sources of nourishment: nature and story. Both subjects: 51 percent.

My moods, lies and need for privacy distanced me from most of my friends and set me up to fall for a boy five years my senior, who was not only a wildly talented jazz musician but also a hermit. He and I would drive out to a place called The Pit, an abandoned gravel quarry where he would skid around on his dirt bike while I sat in his truck pretending to be captivated by him. While he was off exploring some distant berm, I would pull out a sepia-paged book on Renaissance polyphony and try to sing through excerpts of choral works by Palestrina until the sneer of the dirt bike came close and I would slip the book back into my purse and once again admire him dutifully through the window.

No one understood what I saw in him—me, least of all. We never went anywhere except The Pit and his basement—not to a single party, dance, park, movie or restaurant. We didn't get together with friends (he had none and most of mine were estranged), and he refused to meet any member of my family. I never told him about my dad, choosing instead to make up a whopper about him "living with his twenty-year-old secretary in Toronto," which my boyfriend found shocking enough. My mother kept trying to invite him over for dinner, but he categorically dismissed the invitations, telling me, "No offence, but I don't really like parents."

So, whenever my boyfriend came over to my house, he would come only as far as the driveway, where he would sit in his ultra-cool sports car until I noticed him. Then I would drop whatever I was doing (generally teaching myself to play the piano—my new pastime), and we would head to his basement. Aside from the standard necking and fooling around, we would lie in the dark listening to Dave Brubeck, Miles Davis, Herbie Hancock, Chick Corea, Wayne Shorter, Maynard Ferguson and Thelonius Monk. Non-stop, without saying a word to each other, for five to seven hours at a time.

Oh, and we never ate. Anything. And all we ever drank was water. No matter how many mealtimes passed while we were in each other's company. For some reason, he never got hungry and I wouldn't *admit* that I was hungry, perhaps because the one time I did, my boyfriend responded with the admonishing words, "Then you're going to get fat." Which did follow a path of twisted logic, I suppose, because the opposite was certainly true: all this going hours and hours without eating was certainly making me skinny.

While the relationship was odd and I spent much of it starving, those hours we spent together in uncharted, uninhibited musical exploration were ascensions into the wildness craved and required by every adolescent. In societies that have lost their connection to wilderness, teenagers are left to invent it, most often chemically, for themselves. Fortunately, I found it through jazz—not drugs—and those journeys into realms of wild creation fed me in their own way.

The summer before I started grade twelve, my boyfriend moved to Texas to study percussion. After doing the obligatory weeping, I then looked up and smiled for the first time in more than a year. (No doubt my parents were thrilled by the geographical blessing, but neither said a word about it.) Suddenly, I was free to re-create my life: have friends again, eat food, get drunk, have a normal life. I began softening my makeup, plucking my eyebrows, hanging out at parties, eating potato chips, drinking rum and Coke, and dating a football player who loved Barry Manilow. I got round-faced and round-hipped, dizzy with ditsy socializing, and, in the words of my school guidance counsellor, I was "making improvements in adapting to my environment and personal circumstances."

This wouldn't last long.

Words have no sound in alcohol. They are spoken from the bottom of a deep weedy lake. Every time the mouth opens, it fills with water. And so it learns to stay closed. Learns quickly.

I knew nothing in adolescence of the pain behind addiction, only of the lacquered exterior that covered it. I did not know about torrents of unreleased grief, the way they storm and rage in people, filling their bodies with cracks they spend their lives desperately trying to patch. Or that the glaze of alcohol is sorrow-soluble and must be reapplied nightly—and now and again in the afternoon.

I did not see my stepfather as a vessel of saline waters, a body of unshed tears. I did not see his kindness, his effulgent smile, how hard he tried to love life, to love us. Nor did I see how much he wanted us to love him. Through the smug narcissism of adolescence, I saw only a man who had stolen my mother from me and drank too much. And I had no more compassion for my mother, who had taken on something of a shadowed form. Some days I remember seeing her in the house looking wilted and tired and I had no idea who she was.

It wasn't clear how much she had known of Mel's drinking before they were married—it had always been in the context of a party, a vacation, a celebration of their time together. But it was clear that she loved his fun-loving spirit and that he loved hers in return. They travelled, sailed, hiked, played tennis, and I don't know if the drinking got worse over the years or if I simply began to notice it more. But when I watched the two

of them begin dinner as wonderful people and morph into in-
ebriated fools by the end, I felt like reaching across the table
and smashing their heads together.

I tried to talk to my brothers about it a number of times,
but Paul and I spoke very little in those days, and Flip had
descended into an anti-social, Troglodytic existence since the
relocation of the television to the basement.

My stepsiblings and I, comrades in psychedelic Christmases,
remained close, laughing on the phone, launching into friendly
jousting the moment we saw one another, but they lived so far
away that our visits were rare. For a while, when I was sixteen,
the stepbrother with the dreamy eyes came to live with us, and
I remember him as a guiding star in my sky, greeting me every
day when I would return home from school with a mug of hot
chocolate, a fire roaring in the den, and a backgammon board
open and ready for play.

I'm not sure he had any idea of the medicinal value of those
cups of chocolate and fireside games. We never talked about
the atmosphere in the house, the nightly inebriation and the
agony of continually pretending it wasn't happening. In those
months together, we shared a lot of weak smiles and knowing
looks, the occasional tear-lined glance, and each moment of
connection pulled me through to the next day.

That spring, a subdivision of monster homes began to stomp
their way across the fields and forests at the end of our road.
I began to replace inspiring walks in nature with idle and de-
pressing ones in the mall, wandering the shiny, fluorescent-lit

avenues that led me to perfumed delights of every kind. I bought cheap jewellery, a flat iron to tame the wildness out of my mane, a pair of stitched cowboy boots that forced me to change entirely the way I walked, and bags of junk food to scarf on the drive home, where I would then saunter upstairs and bring the whole thing up in the bathroom.

It had been building for a while. Years, I'd say. Hundreds of imperceptible nudges in that direction until one day I found myself there: over the toilet, vomiting food I had just eaten, and feeling so much better, lighter, thinner, emptier— free of knots, tension, lies, deceit, anger, shame, failure, the certainty that my life was Completely Fucked Up, and, last but not least, food.

It was an easy release and an addictive relief, a way to eat and not get fat, get a sugar high and keep my weight low, fall apart but look great, dull my caustic emotions under layers of ice cream and then heave the whole toxic soup out of my body for a while. Generally, just until the next day. Bulimia was my drug, and like the addict who reaches compulsively for the next high, I reached for food, the nearest bathroom, that hor- rifying, disgusting, hate-filled release, and then—fleetingly— the feeling of being okay. Empty. Light.

Free.

And then it would start all over again.

It was like being in a boat with an infuriating crack in its hull. Just when I had finished bailing, it seemed, sometimes only hours afterwards, I would feel the water level start to rise again, that sickening, gnawing anxiety that I knew only one way of calming. And so I would start again. Finish again. Swear it was going to be the last time. And then start again.

I never got skeletal, just perfectly magazine-thin. In this way at least, I was society's ideal.

"You look great!" people said to me in greeting.

And as happy as I was for the stamp of approval, the comment filled me with rage and contempt. I looked *great*? Was everyone so deluded? Could they not *see*?

Actually, a few people could, but the moment they expressed concern—"How *are* you?" "Is everything *okay*?"—I would distance myself, because no one could find out what I was doing, what was really happening, what a disaster I was. The mortification would have killed me. Or so I felt.

I had to get out, get away, start fresh, find my place. Wherever that was. I decided I needed to leave the country. Better still, the continent. To finish school as quickly as possible and move to Europe—to my mind, a mythical paradise.

In the meantime, I tried to stay sane. Stop going to parties. Pass my classes. Save money. Spend time with people like Mary Smithey, my friend from sweeter, more innocent days. And play the piano, which nourished and moved me when little else could.

When we were kids, my brothers and I used to joke that we were the victims of auricular torture: awoken on Saturday mornings to the sound of my mother's students mutilating Mozart à la Suzuki Method. The upside of the torture was that after sixteen years of repetitive listening, I was able to work through the entire series of piano books in a matter of a few months, practising three to four hours a day; on weekends, as much as eight. The music was already there, deep in my cell tissue, so it was just a matter of strengthening my fingers and learning how to move them in the right way to get the music out.

Soon, my mother felt that I was playing well enough to take on some of the students she couldn't accommodate, so carloads of obligated children began to arrive on a weekly basis, music books in hand. I couldn't bear to put even the advanced ones through the tedium of scales and sight-reading (besides, I didn't know how to do either), so I focused instead on getting music into their skin, turning phrases into stories or dances. My students and I all enjoyed each other, we had some good laughs and the odd virtuosic moment, but after a year of lessons, they could no more have passed a conservatory exam than have ridden a camel. I hoped to be out of the country, cash in hand, before any of their parents really noticed.

On weekends, I moonlighted at a country club. As balls went pinging across the rolling, poison-soaked lawns, I served food, some of which was spat upon by the cook or dropped deliberately on the floor before being placed on a plate for the customer who had had the gall to make a special order. We catered an exorbitant number of weddings, all of them so similar I sometimes wondered if the same people were back again. My private goal was to have every plate of dessert hurled onto the tables before the *hardy-har-har* speech about the groom's embarrassing past and the inevitable gush about love and the glories of marriage.

Real love, real life, lay elsewhere. In Europe somewhere. I was convinced of it.

A friend of my mother's knew of a university in France that offered a language program for foreign students, and my mother helped me to apply. My dad thought it was a wonderful idea—sure to be very stimulating—and he pored over maps of France with me, plotting possible weekend getaways, while Lance sat beside us excitedly reading excerpts aloud from the Michelin Guide: France.

The day my letter of acceptance came in the mail—that strange cursive writing and all of those foreign stamps!— I felt a surge of true excitement for the first time in years. I remember my mother sitting at the piano, lifting her hands from the middle of a Rachmaninoff prelude, smiling as I read the letter aloud.

A few months later, at seventeen, having crammed two semesters of high school into one—two dead frogs in one jar, as it were—I packed two suitcases, climbed onto a taut emotional slingshot, and pinged myself to France.

The Plan: I would learn French, find the meaning of life, never go back!

Specifically: I would do the language course. Speak fluently in no time. Then, wander the French countryside until I came to a cobblestone village with terra-cotta tiled roofs, herbs growing wild out of stone walls and a village of people sitting around a long wooden table sharing a baguette. They would look up in the middle of a discussion about Flaubert and smile when I approached, tell me I look terrible—say, *here, darling, have some chocolate*; and ah, mon Dieu, *what a very cultured thing to have a gay father. And a Simone de Beauvoir–type mother, how absolutely marvellous. Here,* chérie, *'ave a glass of Bordeaux.*

Shortly thereafter, a man without a word of English would fall dramatically in love with me, serenading me with baritone arias while scooping me into his arms and carrying me through fields of lavender to a cottage on a hillside. When not being massaged or made love to, I would read beautifully undissected novels under an arched window, sleep under frescoes, and picnic in the shadows of cypress trees. And I would live in that perfect place forever.

None of which happened.

But I did fall in love with France. With walking. With admiring buildings and cobblestones, courtyards and fountains, vistas that made me laugh with sheer pleasure. I loved speaking French. Eating baguettes. Getting quietly chubby and having no one notice or care. When my language course finished, I got a train pass and clackety-clacked around Europe for three months, sleeping in hostels, jumping on and off trains whenever I felt inspired, and filling myself with beauty as I wandered, drawing nourishment from landscapes and languages, free concerts and museums, passing friendships, movable feasts and shared food.

Just before my eighteenth birthday, after six months of living and travelling on my own, I met up with my dad and Lance in Amsterdam. The three of us spent several days wandering arm in arm along the canals, eating *rijsttafel* feasts, and looking at Van Gogh from every angle. I particularly remember the way the artist drew hands. From there, Lance cycled off to Belgium, while my dad and I took the train to Paris and checked ourselves into a lovely tumbledown *pension* with patchy carpeted hallways and thick floral drapery.

There was a lot of museum-visiting. The odd concert. One ballet. But the thing I remember most was that the hotelier brought us breakfast, setting the tray down on the weathered carpet, knocking on our door and then creaking away. We would roll out of bed and open the door to be greeted by the miracle of a hot breakfast under linen, and balance it over to the table by the window.

Dad would pour the coffee, I, the hot milk, and we would begin chatting. Perhaps it was the distance from home, the anonymity of that hotel room, or the new independence I felt after living in a foreign country on my own. Whatever it was, all the questions I had never before had the courage to ask found passage to the surface there, and each one my dad considered carefully before answering with excruciating honesty. Many mornings, we talked so much it was after noon before we got out of our pyjamas.

As we divided up the pastries, passed each other the butter, the jam, he confided the torment he had experienced about his sexual orientation at different points in his life, the anguish he had felt in deciding how to go about living truthfully, how long he had struggled with the question of his being gay. Far longer, I learned (taking a hard gulp of coffee), than I would ever have guessed.

"If I'd been born ten years earlier, it's very possible that I would never have come out at all," he said in response to something I had asked about the timing of it, his being in the vanguard of the gay revolution. "And if I'd been born ten years later, most probably I would never have married."

He paused. Reached over, touched my arm and smiled. "But I'm glad things went exactly as they did," he said, his eyes glistening in the dust-speckled light.

He took a bite of his croissant, a crumble of greasy, golden flakes gathering on his lips and fingers, a few on the cuff of his periwinkle-coloured raw-silk pyjamas. With his eyes closed, he licked each finger dreamily, taking so much delight in that damn croissant that I beamed just watching him.

I began coming out as the daughter of a fairy shortly after those Paris chats. Like many people who come into the truth of themselves, I began by sussing out a few sympathetic people far removed from my world and trying the news out on them. When that wasn't catastrophic, I took note of how good it felt to exhale and be myself, and went from there. Slowly, one person at a time.

Mostly it was easy; people were surprisingly accepting. But I remember in my second year of university seeing an article in the student newspaper about the difficulties of being gay on campus and still being so secretive about my life that I would not even sit at the same table with someone reading that issue. It was the late 1980s, when AIDS was roaring through the gay community and the public perception of gay people was formed largely by images of gaunt, blistered men. Faces that haunted us all. Those were frightening, devastating times. The death toll was immense, impossible to calculate. To contract AIDS was to die. And many of my dad's friends did. I knew who was HIV-positive and I used to watch them at Dad and Lance's dinner parties, wondering how they managed to talk, eat and laugh, knowing a monster was devouring them from within.

One Christmas, Dad invited me to a concert of the Toronto Gay Men's Chorus, a variously talented group that performed a variety of music from Brahms to Broadway. Dad was the conductor. For the choir's finale, he parted the group in two, opening a wide space in the middle of the stage where a long white canvas had been hung. Every man held a candle, the lights dimmed, and Dad conducted the choir in a half-tempo, *pianissimo* performance of "Stille Nacht"— "Silent Night" in its original German.

The stage was dark, save the teardrop flames of the candles and a small spotlight illuminating my dad's dancing arms. As the choir began the second slow verse, slides were projected centre stage: thin, blemished men in hospital beds, gaunt smiling faces surrounded by loved ones; face after face after breaths-from-death face.

"Schlaf in himmliche Ruh'. . ."

Sleep in heavenly peace.

It didn't matter if the faces were familiar or not, the slowness of the tempo allowed everyone who needed to, to sob. Which I did not, though some were faces I recognized. People I knew, but none I had been very close to. And I had not yet learned to share heart the way I do now. Today I would have cried; then I did not.

Until the last verse, when the images changed. To simple scenes of love and celebration: families arm in arm around Christmas trees and dinner tables, athletic men embracing at Pride Day parades, mothers and sons, an older man with a broad smile holding a sign saying PROUD OF MY GAY SON, and then me at age fourteen, cheek to cheek with my dad, arms flung around his neck, the two of us cuddling, all teeth and brown eyes, the same curly dark hair. There were some of my brothers laughing with Dad in the kitchen, then one of all of us, including my mother.

Throughout it all, against the backdrop of the family he had left in order to come into the person he is, my dad was held in a circle of light, his arms sweeping through the air with a conductor's transcendent grace.

In all my life, I had never seen him more beautiful.

PART TWO

The Way He Saw It

SELECTED CONTENTS OF THE BOX:

• a small blue diary

• newspaper clippings from *The Globe and Mail,*
       Toronto Star, Body Politic, Weekend Magazine

• drafts of letters to friends and family

• letters received from friends

• notes to self

• inspiring excerpts from plays

• loose-leaf journal entries

• "My Story"

Excerpts from the small blue diary

1978!
I feel compelled to take up this diary again, to write from the
heart and the gut about the excitement and trepidation of the
last few months, my changing perceptions of where I am and
where I am going. Perhaps by recording this I can find some
release from the churning and re-churning of those events
and thoughts which I dwell on constantly. And, if anyone else
reads this, perhaps they will start to understand my view of
where I am at.

Halifax, 28.6.78
Finally after years of wondering about myself, wanting and
often hoping that someone else would take the initiative, I
have taken it myself. Attending the Association of Canadian
Orchestras Conference in Halifax gave me the opportunity to
do some essential interviewing of Nova Scotia Liberals, but
also to be in the same city where the annual Canadian Gay
Conference was taking place.

For a year or two now, I have walked by gay bars, discos
and baths in Toronto without daring to venture inside. I
have been titillated by *Playgirl* and *Mandate* and have learned
something from the outside by reading *Directions**, *Body Politic*,
and an article about gay capitalism in *Toronto Life* (September
1976). I guess the latter was crucial, as it described in detail
a Toronto gay scene, which I supposed existed, but which

---

* *Directions*: a publication for Canadian gay men

I knew nothing about. Then, there was the article about Michael Lynch as a homosexual father in the *Globe*.* It leapt out of the paper at me, because here was someone with whom I could identify: University of Toronto professor, about my age who looked like a normal, down-to-earth person. He loved his son and wanted to be a good father. He did not see that his being gay made that impossible.

When the ACO conference ended, I attempted to find out where the gay conference was taking place. I wandered around the university without seeing any signs of it, though I passed a couple of men defiantly arm in arm, wearing *Body Politic* T-shirts—a rather unsavoury pair, I thought. Not knowing where to look next, I returned towards the downtown and, in the Public Gardens, caught sight of the B.P. pair again. Tailing them at a discreet distance finally produced utter frustration when they were picked up by friends in a car! I again called a gay-line number at which there had been no answer earlier in the evening and was informed that the social activities were taking place above a German restaurant and at the Turret, a kind of disco club. The German restaurant didn't look very promising, so I ate in one of the Historic Properties restaurants . . . running into some of the people who had stayed on to tidy up loose ends from the ACO conference.

By the time I could tear myself away from them, I was so impatient that I strode straight into the Turret without my usual indecisiveness. But I was nervous as I had my hand stamped and signed a fictitious name in the guestbook. Once

---

* *The Globe and Mail*, March 30, 1978

inside, my head spun as I saw men dancing romantically
with other men. An unattractive, stupid (or drunk) looking
young man asked me to dance and the next couple of minutes
almost turned me into a confirmed heterosexual! However,
building up courage, I asked a rather attractive man to dance
and decided that this sort of thing might be pleasant after
all. After one dance he told me he "couldn't get it together
with me." Whether that referred to my dancing or my body, I
didn't know, but I stayed until the end, thoroughly fascinated
and "turned on."

29.6.78

I was back again the next night and saw a man whom I immediately recognized as Michael Lynch. I introduced myself,
told him how the *Globe* article had made such an impact on me
and asked him if I could talk with him sometime in Toronto.
For the first time in eighteen years, I blurted out to another
human being that I thought I might be gay, though I added
that it would be an awful lot easier if I wasn't. I asked him to
dance, with the nervous confession that I didn't know how
to dance with a man. It was short, but I kept saying to myself,
"I'm dancing with Michael Lynch," and that blew my mind.

30.6.78

Michael had suggested that I come to some of the conference
and after a day interviewing Liberal politicians, I [went and]
listened (at the back of the room!) to a session on the problems of older gays. I was terrified I would see someone I knew

and for a second, thought I saw someone from Trent, but it turned out to be Michael Lynch. The talk was all so strange to me, though a lot of it pertained to the problems of volunteer organizations—political parties and orchestras all over again! Michael's carefully considered, questioning intervention was, to me, reassuringly professional.

I went back to the Turret again that evening and talked with Michael a bit about the sabbatical which he had just completed and some research that he was going to be doing next month, but he seemed very tired and I left early because I had to catch a 6 a.m. plane the next morning.

1.7.78
Michael had told me where to write him and on the trip home I carefully composed a guarded but (so I hoped) affectionate letter, asking him to send me his telephone number.

July/78
I spent the month impatiently looking for Michael's reply in every mail delivery to the university. Bit by bit, I found out that he was out of town for the month. I got his number from B.P. and, after a couple of telephone encounters with his roommate, found him home at last. We arranged an afternoon when I could see him at his house.

August 1978
I must be mad, I kept saying to myself on the bus to Toronto. I am going to tell someone whom I hardly know things about

myself that I have never discussed with anyone. Michael greeted me in a friendly way, though taken aback by the moustache of my new persona. My expectations of a promising friendship rose when I saw a Steinway grand in his living room and was informed that, yes, he did play. I calmed myself down with a couple of Bach preludes while he got lunch for his son and another youngster.

In the garden we had desultory conversation for a minute or two and then I launched forth. I told him about the various male friends to whom I had felt physically attracted, my consuming but unconsummated passion for Stephen [at Oxford]. My disappointment with him, my decision to opt for marriage with the expectation that my homosexual drives would fade (how many men have been misled by that wildly propagated myth?), my affection for Anne and our children, but the disappointment and ultimate sterility of the sexual side of our marriage. (His experience was strikingly similar, even to his wife often having been sick during the first years of their marriage.*) I told him about how all the subjects of my homosexual infatuations invariably turned out to be heterosexual and how I had finally been driven to the point where I had to know, before I was too old for an active gay life, whether sex with a man was really what I thought it might be.

We talked for four hours, walking to a swimming pool, standing under an apartment building out of the rain, at the

---

* My mother became ill shortly after they were married, eventually having both her gall bladder and appendix removed.

pool, in his bank. I was disturbed by the developments in his own life—the dissolution of his marriage, his increasing disinclination to associate with people outside his gay world. I said I was very contented with my straight milieu and hoped I could preserve it. I said, "Do you think I look gay?" and he answered, "Yes, definitely—you're good looking, you're loose and that moustache is very trendy." I felt strangely reassured, even though that appellation was one which I had done everything to avoid for twenty years. In fact, I had believed my "straight" image to have been so successfully nurtured that it explained why I had never been approached by anyone (apart from New Year's Eve 1958*).

It became clear that Michael had no intention of initiating me, but he said, stay at the Carriage House, eat at the Grapes on College, go to the Duke (behind the Park Plaza) and then try the Quest. Again, with fear and trembling, I did everything he suggested and missed (in retrospect through ignorance) a pretty clear lead from an actuary in the Duke. ("Are you cruising?" "No," said I.)

Finally, upstairs at the Quest, I got into conversation with a nice, but not especially good-looking fellow. I told him how all this was new to me. He asked how I liked it. "I do." Then he said, "I like you as a person and I'd like to

---

* On a trip to New York when my father was twenty-one, he was waiting for friends in a bar when he got into conversation with a man who invited him to a place "where men danced with other men." My father remembers being simultaneously excited and terrified. He told the man he was waiting for friends and the man moved on, but my father never forgot the incident.

spend the night with you." "Okay," and he leaned across
the table and kissed me. I warned him that I was a neo-
phyte but he wouldn't believe me. Finally I had to lie and he
seemed reassured.

Skip told me that he was a silversmith and shared a room
with a woman, so we went to my hotel. In the elevator, I had
my first thrilling experience of kissing a stubbly face passionately. Once inside, we made love wildly and without inhibition. It was as if a veil of misunderstanding about my own
self had been ripped away. Stripped and without his glasses,
Skip was very attractive. When we had finished, he showered
and left, saying that he often went to Dudes. Alone, I was
surprised to discover that I wasn't afflicted with the guilt feelings which I had always feared would follow my first sex with
a man. Instead, it was as if a huge oppressive load had been
lifted from me.

10.8.78
I called Michael, thanked him and told him I had done everything he had suggested and had had a marvellous time. Back
in Peterborough, I had a cello lesson, but could barely take in
what J was saying.

11.8.78
Attended orchestras' meeting in Kingston; had a glorious
swim with JG in Lake Ontario; longed to tell him about what
happened on Wednesday, but didn't dare!

24.8.78

Not having much success in the bars in Toronto, I plucked up my courage to try the baths on Mutual Street. It was mind-boggling to see the endless parade of naked men with towels around their middles, circulating back and forth with hardly a word, looking at each other and peering into the little rooms with opened doors. I was not getting very far until I went into the top-floor room with the bunk beds and sat beside a trim blond from Buffalo. His body and especially his tongue were exquisite and delicious. How rude of me afterwards to have to dash off and catch my bus—and we never even exchanged first names. The delights of that experience haunted me for weeks afterwards.

28.8.78 to 2.9.78

I take Alison and Flip to September Camp.* What a power-ful reinforcement of my existing lifestyle seeing all those old friends, especially the Snells.† But is this really me? Was it ever? I don't know.

---

* "Family week" at Camp Ahmek in Algonquin Park

† My father first met John Snell when they were both counsellors-in-training at Camp Ahmek. John was, in my father's recollection, "the first guy I had ever met who was unashamedly interested in the arts, but not a weirdo." They are still good friends today.

Clipping: "A Homosexual Father: many consider him unfit, but 'I love my son,'" The Globe and Mail, *March 30, 1978*

"I'm a gay father," Michael Lynch said. "And there are more of us around than you realize."

Mr. Lynch shares custody of his 6-year-old son with his estranged wife, whom he married eight years ago to "follow the mob."

Today, the University of Toronto English professor is an "out-of-the-closet gay." He separated from his wife nearly a year ago and lives with his boyfriend and his son.

Mr. Lynch and his boyfriend don't hesitate to show their fondness for each other in front of the little boy, who has been told that "daddy is a faggot."

Mr. Lynch, a youthful 37, knows that many consider him unfit to be a parent because he is homosexual. "But I love my son . . . it seems so simple to me," he said.

He spoke with frustration about his reaction to a recent county court decision giving a Montreal father, a self-professed homosexual, custody of his two children.

Mr. Lynch scoffed at County Court Judge Elmer Smith's stress in his Jan. 16 judgment that the Montreal father is worthy of having his children live with him, in part, because he is "discreet . . . has never exhibited any missionary attitude or inclination towards militancy in this difficult area . . . disclaims ownership in any homosexual club . . . doesn't indulge in exhibitionistic behaviour in the presence of the children."

"These things are not at all relevant," Mr. Lynch said. He and his lover hold hands, kiss and hug just as heterosexual couples do. Yet he has the same concern that many partners have about "being too intimate in front of the children."

"I am completely open with my son. Children should know from the beginning. He hears the word 'gay' all the time and he has questioned. . . . I explain to him it means wanting to be with boys and having especially close relationships with boys."

Mr. Lynch is politically active in the homosexual rights movement, writing occasional articles for the homosexual rights publication *Body Politic*; acting as chairman of the committee to defend John Damien (a race steward dismissed in 1975 by the Ontario Jockey Club because he is a homosexual); and doing research on issues affecting homosexuals at the university. He taught the university's first homosexual studies course and is on sabbatical to write a book about homosexual poets.

Although these activities might be considered militant, Mr. Lynch is convinced that they will not harm his son or turn him into a homosexual.

"Look, I was exposed to aggressively heterosexual parents for 18 years of my life. They did everything they could to turn me into a heterosexual. Nothing I do can turn my son into a homosexual."

The father acknowledges his sexuality will have some effect on his son.

The boy won't suffer because of his father's homosexuality, but he will suffer as a result of society's distaste for it, Mr. Lynch said.

"I think a gay parent, like a Pakistani or black parent, has an obligation to prepare the child for the hate that he'll be taught at school. Schools, churches, society, newspapers teach this hate and one has to say, 'Look, be ready—your daddy is a faggot.'

"He knows I suffer and have fears about all kinds of social hate. I tell him. I don't know how much he understands fully. He may have some tough moments growing up, but so does a Pakistani child, and you wouldn't take that child from a loving parent because a swastika has been painted on his door."

Mr. Lynch said he hopes to transmit to his son "a bitterness against a society which is sexist. I want him to have a kind of bitterness or strong rejection of those standards."

He also wants his son to understand that men, whatever their sexual orientation, can be affectionate, tender and loving with men and women. "He is not going to be a super-macho male. He's not going to feel because he's male he has to be rigid and distant or authoritarian."

Mr. Lynch laughs at curiosity about how a homosexual can be a parent. He says the public would be surprised at how many homosexual parents there are if every homosexual stood up and told the truth.

He has organized a discussion group of eight homosexual parents of varied marital statuses and custody situations and knows of three Toronto homosexuals involved in custody cases. . . . In his own case, Mr. Lynch and his wife will divorce and are planning to arrange joint custody of their son.

Excerpts from the small blue diary

14.9.78

Michael had told me about various discussion groups including one called Married Gays. Its extreme confidentiality appealed to me and so I found myself, very nervously, ringing a (coded) doorbell in a smart new apartment block not far from the C.N. Tower and the Royal Alex. The host was Stan Wild, a fiftyish, grammar-school Englishman who is very devoted to the gay social service system.

This is my first introduction to the incredible array of situations one finds in talking with gay men. Warren and Jim didn't look gay *in the least*. Warren in his late fifties has a kind of sexy self-assuredness. He has teenaged children and claims he never had *any* gay inclinations until two years ago. He is sure his wife doesn't know about his affairs, but says their sex life has really fallen off.

According to Jim, *his* wife has always known he was gay, even before they were married. Every so often, he feels the old urge returning, he picks up someone off the street, but he feels guilty afterwards. He is a big strapping fellow who looks like he would have been a typical student of the sixties. I talk about how this is all so new to me and I don't know where it is going to lead. It is comforting just to talk it through and to hear about other men and situations.

28.9.78

I have surveyed most of the gay bars in the downtown area.
Either they are not very conducive to meeting people and
chatting with them—there is movement but too much loud
music; or the men appear to sit riveted at their tables for hours
on end. Buddy's is for me, a happy mixture—lots of moving
about, lots of opportunity to engage in casual conversation.

This evening, I leave Buddy's alone and continue my
search at Richmond Street without much success. But as I am
leaving, I meet George, a homely but sort of endearing lawyer
who comes back to the Carlton Hotel with me. His approach
is matter-of-fact. It is after experiences like this that I think
maybe I could just quietly give it all up and carry on with my
Peterborough life, which, incredibly, is so much like it has
always been. But *can* I choose? I don't know.

12 to 15.10.78

I am in Toronto for Contact/78.* I arrive raring to go—and
go directly to Mutual Street where I am immediately picked
up by a sexy Italian, Armand. He compliments me on looking
Italian and on all sorts of other things—what a change
from two weeks ago. Before I know it I am in a threesome
with a man from Calgary—fantastic. After the evening
session of Contact, Gerry and I get together. He turns out

---

* A showcase sponsored by the Ontario Arts Council to give young musicians
the opportunity to perform before representatives of arts organizations that
might engage them. My father was representing Town & Gown, a classical concert
series he organized in Peterborough.

to be something of a fascist and not very passionate. We spend an unproductive night together. Somewhere through the weekend, I also met a computer programmer from Goderich(!), good-looking, but pretty officious once we had finished what we had set out to do. On leaving the establishment, I caught sight of him fully dressed—transformed into a regular Milquetoast!

On Saturday morning, over breakfast at Le Petit Gourmet, I met a fabulously attractive man by the name of Colin. I know that he lives in the area, but unfortunately we parted without my having established certain important pieces of information. One of those delicious but maddeningly ambiguous experiences such as Isherwood writes about in *A Single Man*.

Saturday evening, I go to Katrina's, a sumptuous, but slightly glittery disco-bar. I am somewhat startled to meet John S. and a few others from Contact. I leave fairly early and, on my way back to the Park Plaza, John catches up to me and invites me up to the apartment where he is staying. I go up but decide that I will excuse myself after due proprieties.

John, however, turns out to be a persuasive and sensuous man. We have great sex all over the living room and then do a lot of talking. He is one month older than I am and has been married for twenty years. His wife went through a bad period when she discovered a letter from John's current lover but, in the end, she decided she would rather have him as he is than not to have him at all. Incredibly, he now has a lover who lives just a few houses away and who, John claims, is quite accepted by his wife. He has great sex with both, he says. All of this reassures me in a way because *anything* seems possible. But we part with the warning that I have pain ahead of me.

What an erotic weekend!

I almost forgot about having coffee with Arthur Motyer.* He gave me the sad news that he and Sarah were separating because she disapproves of his bisexual activities. I longed to tell him my story but somehow couldn't decide how to begin.

27.10.78

I went to Toronto for a conference on "Social Upheaval in Italy" and *Don Giovanni* in the evening. At Buddy's afterwards, I talked with an attractive American bookseller from near Chicago. He is married and when he told his wife about being gay, she said simply that she had always suspected he was. He travels a lot and confines his gay activities to out-of-town, but that unfortunately did not include me. Still it was reassuring to chat with another married gay—but what an assortment of situations there are.

After Buddy's, I continued my cruising at Dudes—an after-hours bar. I chatted with two U of T profs who had also been to *Don Giovanni* and then suddenly spied DG from Trent through the crowd—my first direct connection with Peterborough. We both talked openly of the excitement of our

---

* A dear friend of my father's, Arthur was a professor of English and drama, and an inspiring and influential figure to many of his students, among them Michael Ondaatje, who credits Arthur as being the person who first encouraged him to consider dedicating himself to writing.

gay lives, but also how we both liked the calm and security
of a heterosexual existence. He is going to be moving back in
with Carol again—he seems to be in as much of a quandary
as I am.

4.11.78
I go to Toronto for a concert in the Festival series. Armed
with an extra ticket, I drop into Buddy's in hopes of finding
some company. That turns out to be Claude, a psychologist at
University of Waterloo. He is very keen about music, married
with teenage children. He confines his gay life to monthly
visits to Toronto and elsewhere when he attends meetings. All
very compartmentalized. He invites me up to his room in the
Carlton Hotel and what transpires is pretty perfunctory.

It is after this that I go through a period of being rather
depressed about where all this is taking me. All of these
casual encounters seem to be leading nowhere. What I really
want is a male friend in the line of close male friends, which
I have had over the years . . . but what I desperately want now
is a close male friendship, which, for the first time is also a
gay friendship.

I go to the first meeting of a gay fathers' group in
Toronto, partly to have an excuse for seeing Michael Lynch,
but also in hopes of meeting someone. Once again, there is
an incredible array. One comes from a family of five brothers, four of whom are gay. His wife knows and her acceptance
seems to fit into a general pattern which they both have of
fighting for minority causes. The most extraordinary is an

extremely good-looking doctor who relates that, just as he was working up the courage to tell his wife, she, an international model, informed him, after the birth of their second son, that she was a lesbian.

Excerpts from "Forgotten Fathers,"
Michael Lynch, Body Politic, *April 1978*

Preparing this article, I asked about twenty fathers if they could be pictured here with their child or children. Almost all turned me down. They felt that being known as gay would entail a large risk of losing their children through the efforts of homophobic relatives, social workers or judges.

"The numbers of them weren't all that impressed me," Brian Miller (who is conducting a sociological study of gay fathers in the U.S. and Canada) recounts. "There was also an intensity of experience that I'd not expected." He described instance after instance where a father had broken into tears recalling the pain of having to decide between being honest about his gayness and getting to keep his children. "Every father I've talked with experiences a gap between his life as a father and his life as a gay man. As a parent he is part of his children and they of him; as a gay man he finds that the available social structures discourage the presence of children—or exclude them flatly." The invisibility is due not only to the homophobia of the non-gay world, but also to the failure of other gay men to make a place for children within their world as well.

Surely, one might think, a gay activist experiences this differently, does not feel such a gap. Surely the gay movement has made room for these men.

"Not at all," says Maurice Flood. . . . Maurice is a gay leader in Vancouver and is the father of Isabel, 5, and Margaret, one-and-a-half. Maurice has chosen to live the life of what Don Mager, in a pioneering essay published in 1973, called the "faggot father": "A faggot father is not simply a faggot who at some point fathered a child, but more significantly he is a man whose sexual orientation is gay and whose daily life includes an active participation in the lives of his children."

Maurice and Cynthia Flood live in a large house with two other gay men. All four adults have been active in feminist, left and/or gay politics. One might expect that such a context would make being a faggot father easier. But here's what Maurice has to say:

"The out-of-the-closet gay father is looked upon by heterosexuals and even by gays as a slightly ridiculous, bizarre creature. He doesn't fit any current conventional pattern of behaviour and in that sense is considered weird and unacceptable. Many gays, particularly in the gay movement, regard parenthood as a retrograde step. The out gay father is seen as someone who has not quite rejected or escaped the family. . . . The status of the out gay father is a lonely one, particularly in the gay community."

• • •

John Lee of Toronto has been out to his daughter and son since they were four and two, respectively. Now 18 and 16, they have grown up comfortable in knowing

their father's sexuality. . . . "The single most important factor in being a good parent," John says, "is being
honest. My children have never had trouble with my
living with men, though of course they have liked some
more than others." He counsels gay fathers to come out
as early as possible. "If you tell children more than they
can understand, they'll let you know," he says. "So I
prefer to exceed rather than underestimate their com-
prehension. Children are remarkable in their attention
and understanding. At an early age they won't understand physical acts—heterosexual or homosexual—but
they will understand affection, struggles, anger, tenderness. They can sense it, and resent it, when a parent is
dishonest with them."

Above all, the problem facing the forgotten gay
father is the spectre of isolation. Gay men may no
longer be invisible, but gay fathers remain so. Like all
subminorities, they suffer a more intense version of
the general oppression experienced by the minority as
a whole. Upon learning that I'd talked with other gay
fathers, one almost shouted, "Where on earth did you
find them?" The hunger to share experience is one that
any gay person who has been isolated would understand. So would any parent who has been isolated from
other parents. Parenthood, like sexuality, becomes a
crucial component in one's sense of oneself.

"There's a lot I'd like to talk about with another gay
father," one man told me, "but there's no place to do it.

In the parent association at school we're not out to one another, if there even are any other gay parents there. And I feel completely apart from straight parents. In the bars there's an unwritten rule against talking about something like parenthood, except as an oddity."

"My loneliest hours," another said, "are those in the park while the boys are playing. I'd like to be with another gay adult then, to talk over the week's discoveries and decisions. I watch the heterosexuals who meet there to chat while their children play—but I'm alone."

• • •

Two days ago eight gay fathers, and three of our children, gathered for the first time, and I found in that group a sense of commonality I'm not used to among gay men. "Being a parent," one of them said, "is a more engulfing experience than just being married or being gay—we are bound to have much more in common." All of us are battling sexism, both Out There and within ourselves. In each other's presence, we eight were no longer forgotten fathers.

Where do we go from here?

Letter from Arthur Motyer, a former colleague and friend from
the mid-1960s, to my father; handwritten on the letterhead of Mount
Allison University, where Arthur taught for twenty-three years

Monday, Nov. 27th, 1978

My dear Joe,

    "Does any of this surprise you?"

    No, not really. My intuition has proven a pretty reli-
able guide over the years; but since you are not the conventional stereotype (the sort society thinks to exist and
rarely does) any more than, I hope, I am, I could not be
sure. I *was* sure, when I told you my story, that you would
understand, but I did not wish to press the point about
yourself. I felt the time would come when you would
tell me something, but I didn't know when. Thank you
now for your trust. I'm glad I made it possible for you to
share this with me.

    But, dear, dear Joe, how strange life is in all its
unfoldings! Can we believe it is unfolding as it should?
I look back now and understand more clearly why it is
we have always had a special kind of bond and how it
is we have always been able to be quickly in tune with
each other, even after gaps of years. In my intuitive way I
knew this about you before you were married; but I never
thought you were dishonest in marrying (which Sarah
now accuses me of being), for exceptional people (and I
think you and Anne *are* exceptional) can sometimes cope

and make such a marriage successful. Yet I wondered. And I wondered for years about you, and I wondered while I was talking to you the other day. Still, I think you were right *NOT* to mention it then. That was *my* moment. Now is *your* moment.

Of course I have no advice for you. If you are in such a group as you are in in Toronto, that is probably help enough. Yet I may have some special insights since I've been through so much myself and because I know you *and* Anne.*

I would assume that you and Anne could work out a *modus vivendi* in a way Sarah and I cannot, and I say that because Anne has long had an interior quality which sustains her (or seems to) apart from you. She is thus *her own person* and may, because of it, be able to come to terms with you. If you honestly try to recognize the quality of yourself and come to terms with that, then I believe you are (one is) in a better position to come to terms with others. . . .

When it comes down to it, I probably don't know Anne all that well. Our relationship has been a surface one of fun . . . . but I suspect she doesn't need *you* to be herself a secure person in her own right. If you want a *modus vivendi*, you have, therefore, a good chance to work on something from such a base. You might just think about that.

I told Sarah before we were married, but I suppose I thought I was "over it," and she has a view that all of

---

* Arthur and his wife had two children.

this is a lot of immoral (not to mention "illegal" when you're married) nonsense; and all a man needs is good old heterosexual sex enough times to make him see the light. Of course it doesn't work that way. But her greater *knowledge* of me, over the last 10 years, has not brought with it a greater *understanding* of me, and that is the sad thing. With you, it might work differently.

But do you want to stay married? With a wife's understanding (and it takes an unusual woman) it *can* work as an extra dimension *within* a marriage and not just a rigid alternative to it. It seems to me there is some chance that Anne might see it this way.

I did not mean to get onto yet another page. You will tire of all my words. But how I wish I could see you! There is no chance before Christmas (unless you are in New York between Dec. 15th and 21st), but I shall look for an excuse early next year to visit Toronto. In the meantime, please write again and feel free to discuss anything you like with me, knowing there's a fair chance I will understand.

But you intrigue me! Whom did you meet last weekend in Toronto? Someone I know? Not Robertson Davies, I hope. The social fabric really would crumble. . . .

Write again soon. I think of you.

Love, A

Handwritten draft of a letter from
my father; undated and unfinished

Dear Arthur,

Thanks very much for your warm, understanding and very perceptive letter, which I received today. I think you are right about Anne and it could very well be that because we have never been completely dependent on each other, we could incorporate this new dimension. She *does* have self-reliance and an inner toughness that allow her to be her own person. On the other hand, I would dread bearing the brunt of that toughness!

Who is my friend? It's all quite extraordinary, as he himself said. It was one of those classic encounters—we exchanged first names, where we were from. We had such great fun and lovely banter—not the usual sort of "serious business." Then later (much later) in the evening, I suddenly thought—I know that face—Richard? Stratford? "Your last name wouldn't be Monette, by any chance?"*

The embarrassing thing is that I have never seen him in anything, though as I said at the time, I would bet he hadn't read any of my political articles either!

We had another marvellous time together on Friday—dinner, chamber music concert (he confesses

---

* At the time, Richard Monette was a well-known Canadian actor and director; he would later become known for his fourteen-season tenure as artistic director of the Stratford Shakespeare Festival of Canada (1994–2007).

not to know much about music but is very receptive), a few drinks, etc. Once again, such fun. However, he is concerned that my marital status makes it impossible for us to carry on. He is afraid of the complexities and wants a lover who can live with him in Stratford and obviously I can't fill that bill.

I felt very sad afterwards because it seemed we had really clicked. We left agreeing that we could both do some thinking and meet again, at least to talk. Your doubts about whether the world is unfolding as it should are so well founded! I told Richard I was not surprised by what he said, that it would be so much easier if he had turned out to be a lawyer or a high school teacher in Peterborough. I would suspect that he is headed for even bigger things and I can understand that with his life he needs a personal anchor. The mind boggles at the possible complexities, but I hate to see the whole thing drop!

I didn't feel that our relationship had to be a deep, dark secret. In fact, I told Anne that I was seeing Richard for the evening and would be staying overnight with him. I guess his portrayal of Hosanna* gave him a certain notoriety (though he has had some important "straight" roles at Stratford since then), but what the hell if people want to draw conclusions. I am not prepared to eat crow—even though the circumstances *are* indeed what they might appear! We did talk vaguely about him

---

* *Hosanna* by Michel Tremblay features a flamboyant transvestite in the title role, one of the first openly gay characters in Canadian theatre.

spending a short time at Trent as an artist-in-residence before rehearsals begin at Stratford and about the possibility of spending part of my sabbatical together—but the latter is, at this stage, of course, premature.

I have felt very sad about this and it is great to be able to talk about it in a letter, even though I am sure you have no ready answers. Do you in fact know Richard? He is terribly nice and not the sort of bizarre type one might have expected.

Spoof on William Shakespeare's "Polonius's
Farewell to Laertes" from Hamlet, *Act I;*
written by my father on his manual typewriter

Give thy coq no vin,
To any well proportion'd coq, thy back.
Be thou familiar, but only in backrooms vulgar;
The tricks thou'st had, when of their performance tired,
Grant them as they go, thy heaps of thanks;
Then duly fill thy palm with entertaining
Some new-hatch'd, untired comrade. Beware
Of entering old queens; but, being in,
Bear't that th'old crow may be aware of thee.
Give every man thine ear, if that's his choice;
Take each man's caresses and so make thy judgment.
Costly thy habit, if that's how thou gett'st thy kicks,
But, hotly press'd, by a fancy, bitchy body,
Beware, lest th'apparent softness proclaims a sham,
And they in France can often cause frustration,
Being most neglect in gender; watch for that!
Either a bugger, or a buggee be;
But buggee oft exposes himself to infection,
And buggering dulls the interest in husbanding.
This above all: to thine orientation be true,
And it must follow that, night after night,
Thou canst not then be false to any man.

Handwritten draft of a letter from
my father, undated and unfinished

Dear Richard,

I was very saddened by our talk just before we parted
on Friday night. I can quite understand your assess-
ment that our continued involvement would probably
be complex and difficult and not really what either of us
would see as ideal. As I told you, I have had a number of
very close male friendships—most of whom are still close
friends even though of necessity we may not see each
other for months or years at a time—but without a sexual
consummation (which I now admit I would have liked).

When, a short time ago, I accepted and began to
act on my being gay, the opposite was presented—lots
of sex but all one-night stands. While mostly lots of fun
at the time, I have increasingly felt that I didn't want to
go on indefinitely in that routine. That is why I enjoyed
meeting you so very much. Not only was our sex sen-
sational (for me, anyway), but I really enjoyed our little
banter and our chat afterwards. You were so much fun
to be with and here at last was someone whom I had
much in common with. For me, that was all delightfully
confirmed on Friday.

I think there are also several things I should make
clear about my situation here. First of all, I accept as
inevitable that people are going to at least *suspect* that I
am gay. I would *rather* have that than attempt to keep it

all a closely guarded secret. I do know that for some, it wouldn't be such a great surprise in any case. I would prefer to avoid dramatic revelations (who the hell makes a great point of declaring themselves heterosexual?!), but to let it gradually become apparent—and I include my family in that. Perhaps I made too big a thing out of telling you, before we saw my Peterborough friends at the concert, that I have a "straight" life in Peterborough. It was just that I wanted to avoid *you* being taken by surprise. (I guess I assumed that you hadn't remembered *anything* I'd told you the first time we met—very rude of me!)

I had made a point of telling my wife that I was going to the concert with you and would be staying overnight with you, though obviously I was no more explicit than that. How much she is aware of I just don't know though I would have thought that, if anything, my sexual performance at home ought to have aroused suspicions. In the end I don't know whether she will be prepared to accept a gay husband (I have been amazed to find out that some do).

On the other hand, I don't want to be a Dr. Jekyll in Toronto and Mr. Hyde in Peterborough (or is it vice versa?!) into the distant future and I am quite prepared to face the consequences—though it shouldn't be said that I look forward to it.

So where does that leave us? I would hate to think that just as we were getting to know each other, the whole thing was over—fine. I guess I understand your wanting a lover who can live with you in Stratford and, ideally, I guess that is what I would want too—though in your case it's a lot bloody more likely!

This is all so new to me and there may very well be other reasons why you wouldn't want our relationship to develop. That I can accept, albeit with reluctance. What would be most sad would be to think that the relationship was being snuffed out because of the practical problems—admittedly they are very real. Where is your sense of adventure?—to be just a bit facetious. And don't forget what I said, just before we said good night on Friday. I do have a whole year off starting this summer.

Excerpts from the small blue diary

8.12.78

Dot, Karen* and I got together for our annual mutual
Christmas present—dinner and show at Second City. After
we got back to the hotel, I excused myself ostensibly to get
something to eat, but really to attempt expunging Richard
from my memory. I headed straight for Mutual Street and,
after several miscues, met Steve, a bearded twenty-two-year-
old. Up in the attic again, the diversion was great, though can
I ever forget Richard? Several days later, I was shocked and
angered to learn that another bathhouse was raided at precisely the same time I was at Mutual Street—what a close call.

16.12.78

With the prospect of a long Christmas vacation ahead of me,
I seized one last chance to run off to Toronto, ostensibly to do
some Christmas shopping, but also to see the San Francisco
Gay Collective do the show *Crimes Against Nature*. All the
characters struck me as being very caricatured—the thing
the gay movement always complains about and not nearly as
moving as the film *Word Is Out*.

6.1.79

Christmas with the Soanes and Neufelds† and New Year's

---

* Dot's daughter, my father's niece; my father had yet to tell them that he was
gay.

† my mother's family

with the Cranes, Hennigers and Aykroyds* are happy occasions, but I cannot help wondering what the circumstances will be a year from now.

I go through a period of feeling very lonely and frightened about the future and I decide I have to make contact with someone in Peterborough. I decide on Lee Beach as an old friend, even though I haven't seen much of him recently. Getting up the nerve to make a move is comical. I circle round and round Traill College on my bicycle, I go into Traill, walk by Lee's office and, to my terror, find him in. But I walk right by his office, get on my bicycle and ride off. Enough of this nonsense, I know I want to make a move, so back I go.

I arrange to come to Lee's apartment the beginning of the next week. As I go to see him, deciding on my opening words is difficult. I conclude that I cannot start off by asking him if he is gay, I have got to tell him, however briefly, what has happened to me before I have a right to ask him anything. That is in fact what happens before I blurt out—you and Gus *are* a gay couple, aren't you.

Lee laughs—I'm sure that's what everyone at the university thinks, Gus and I are both gay, but we are just good friends. In fact, Gus is disgusted that anyone could think he was sexually attracted to someone skinny like me! Lee and I have a good chat—he tells me he had not "come out" until he was 38 (I was astonished) and how his first soured love affair had sent him to a psychiatrist. However, he can't really give

---

* friends of my parents in Peterborough

me any advice on the question—how does a gay man survive in Peterborough without constantly running off to Toronto?

27.1.79

I am alternately depressed and sanguine about my situation—my moods being influenced by the ups and downs of my affairs—and lack of them. . . . Should I tell Anne and get it over with, no matter what happens? Back in August, I told Michael Lynch that I was basically very happy in my heterosexual world—now I wouldn't say that. . . .

Again, I keep thinking about my family and decide that, in any case, Anne could quite conceivably tell me that she didn't want to know anything about my gay life if I were to broach the subject with her. The sexual aspect of our marriage has never amounted to much and has dwindled away completely. I had already decided that I was not going to make a great effort to cover my tracks and I now decide that the strategy I will adopt is to answer truthfully any questions she asks, but not to volunteer any more information than necessary. I don't want to deceive and perhaps this is the best way of achieving the best sort of balance. Lately I have become so aware of the fact that each marriage is unique and perhaps this is the most appropriate course for ours.

Handwritten notes on lined paper

— have come out to a few gay friends, joined Gay
   Fathers of Toronto
— periodically engulfed with trepidation for the future
— fear estrangement from children, but want to be
   able to teach them about homosexuality, help them
   with the problems they will encounter in their own
   adolescence
— have been amazed how, on the surface, life carries on
   as before
— have decided to let my family know gradually—
   neither secretive nor deceptive
— prepared for the truth to come out sometime, but
   sometimes the waiting is more than I can bear
— also not sure how long I want to go on with my foot
   in both camps
— desperately want a dear friend, who is also a sexual
   partner—what I wanted of the last 25 years, but was
   afraid to seek
— torn between the unpredictable search for a lover,
   the intense but perhaps ephemeral sexual pleasure
   which I crave, and the less intense, but perhaps more
   dependable, more deeply satisfying happy home life
   as husband and father. Are these really the choices?
   Can I really choose? I suspect not. Perhaps, after all,
   we are all just like small boats on an often turbulent,
   always swelling sea, constantly working just to keep

underway and afloat, and catching our pleasures when
they come in sight
— my moods change wildly, even within a day—at
times my home life is a cage, at other times a precious refuge which I want to cling to as long as I can

Why do we have to endure such pain?

Clipping: Letters to the Editor,
Toronto Star, *January 20, 1979*

I have traced back my first remembered homosexual impulse to the age of 7. From the age of 12 I was having frequent erotic fantasies about men. When I was 14 I discovered the word *homosexual* in a book, and learned from the same book that I was sick, disgusting and evil; I grew up with the assumption that was how my parents would see me, if they knew. I was unable even to tell anyone about myself until I was 25, my shame was so deep. I went through my life in a state of perpetual tension, anxiety and guilt.

I got married, raised three children, and passed through the hands of four different psychiatrists in my efforts to be "cured."

I am now in my 40s, with a broken marriage and a lot of heartbreak—my wife's as well as my own—behind me.

I have accepted that I am homosexual; I am happy, confident, well-adjusted, and on very good terms with my many students, all of whom must know about me; I proudly wear a Gay Rights button to my classes.

At last, I recognize that I am neither sick, disgusting nor evil. I am functioning more creatively, as writer and teacher, than ever before in my life.

My children, who live in England, know all about my situation, and have accepted it without difficulty;

they are coming over to spend the summer with me and my lover. Children are not harmed by sexual knowledge; they are harmed by the attitudes of disgust and shame that many adults force upon them.

With my background of a childhood, adolescence and manhood of prolonged and pointless anguish, I am deeply grateful to Mayor John Sewell for his official acknowledgement of my right to be regarded as human.*

Those who oppose him might well ponder my case. The misery I have experienced, the misery I have caused, were both the direct result of the oppression of homosexuals within our culture.

Those parents who are so concerned about their children might pause to think that they may be helping to impose on them the misery and guilt that were imposed on me. My parents never knew that I was homosexual, either, for how could I tell them?

Robin Wood

Chairman

Department of Fine Arts

York University

---

* Newly elected mayor John Sewell attended a Free the Press rally for *Body Politic* after it had been charged with using the mail to distribute "immoral, indecent or scurrilous" material; it was later found not guilty. Mayor Sewell made a speech at the rally in which he called for the legal protection of gays.

Excerpts from the small blue diary

20.3.79

Looking back over the last several months, I would judge my emotions to be on a more even keel. That unrestrained drive to experiment—or simply to experience—that I felt in the first few months has subsided. Even my gay life has settled into a pattern: Gay Fathers of Toronto dinners every two or three weeks, the occasional overnight stay in the city, the odd chat with Ian Chapman.* On the other side of things, my home life continues to go on placidly.

I have a feeling that Anne realizes something and silently accepts—but perhaps that is wishful thinking. Since 9.2.79, I have met two very pleasant men—Hank, a linguistics prof at U of T, recently separated from his wife who lives in Ottawa with their two boys; he cooks, sails, loves nude sunbathing and talks about his recent gay life as an exciting adventure— Hank displays an honest effervescence—he admits to pining still after his first love, an R.C. priest, and I tell him I know how it feels. We also have a dislike of the one-night stand. We hit it off well, and Hank tells me that he would love to ask me back to his apartment, but he has hurt his arm (it turns out later to be broken) and lovemaking is just too painful, but we agree to keep in touch and he is interested in GFT.

The other man is Robin Wood who had written a splendid letter to the *Star* during the Sewell–*Body Politic* trial period. I had written to him and said that I hoped we might meet

---

* a gay friend and colleague from Trent University; later a roommate in Toronto

sometime—not the least because of our common interest in the arts. He answered and suggested we meet for a drink sometime. We met in the Duke in the Eaton Centre and hit it off well. Most of the time we talked about music and the Beethoven Fourth Symphony he is reviewing for *Fugue,* but we also compared our family experiences—he was married and has three children.

Robin loved his wife, but, in the end, she couldn't bear the thought of sharing him and he moved out. Shortly afterwards, I gather, he came to Canada and became Fine Arts Chairman at York. Robin has a beautiful manner which suggests he is at peace with himself and in his letter to the *Star* he talks about his past distress—4 psychiatrists and a marriage breakup—but now he happily accepts his being gay. I feel I would like to know Robin better and he asks me to keep in touch.

Meeting people like Robin and Hank leads me to conclude that there are lovely people in this new world—but how strange to share with other men as friends this terribly important, at times difficult experience, but at the same time, to see them as sexually attractive, possible lovers or disappointments.

26.3.79

I had a call from a guy called Don who spoke furtively, said we shared the same "problem," called himself a friend of Robin Wood and asked if he would see me. We met the next day—unfortunately a pretty ordinary looking fellow, though remarkably well preserved. He told me his pathetic story. He has been actively gay for about seven years and felt so guilty about his first encounter that he told his wife. He had a Trent prof as a lover for a year or more and was shattered when that broke up.

He seems to hate his life, but is too timid to break out of it and he seems to hate himself for being gay—last Christmas he said he tried to commit suicide. He is desperate for companionship and I suggested the Gay Fathers group, but he said it would be too much of a hassle for him to explain to his wife why he was going to Toronto.

I said I thought he had to decide what he really wanted. A sad case—he is caught between two worlds. In some ways, our situations are similar, except that I have accepted with joy and relief that I am gay. I tried to tell Don how, unexpectedly, I found that gay men were warm, supportive, interesting, and that one could be glad one was gay.

Clipping: "Homosexuality Can Be Traced to Infancy,"
The Globe and Mail, *April 26, 1979*

Homosexual tendencies are created in infancy and early childhood by the parents' earliest reactions to their offspring, a U.S. expert on adolescent sexuality said yesterday.

Dr. Paul Fink said it is a myth that a seduction by someone of the same sex during adolescence creates homosexuality. What happened in the first 18 months of life is much more important.

Dr. Fink, chairman of the department of psychiatry at Thomas Jefferson University Medical College in Philadelphia, spoke to about 40 doctors specializing in children's problems during a conference organized by the American Academy of Pediatricians.

He said a study by Dr. Robert Stoller of the University of California in Los Angeles shows that a child's "gender identity"—the sense of maleness or femaleness—is established within the first 18 months of life by the infant's relationship with its mother.

A mother typically treats a boy differently from the way she treats a girl, as though he were a bit alien, the study found. If a boy had the sort of close relationship that girls have with their mothers he would want to be a girl.

Dr. Fink said the implication of this and other studies is that a person's sense of gender and choice of a different sex or their own sex as love objects is really determined in infancy. Almost as important as the relationship with the mother in early infancy is the relationship between the child and father during the years from age 3 to 6, Dr. Fink said.

"The father takes the existing gender identity of both the boy or girl and reinforces it by his attitude. For the boy he provides an identification person. The boy wants to grow up to be just like him. . . . The little girl needs a father available to affirm her femininity."

Dr. Fink said homosexuality is not a disease but a case of arrested development. The male homosexual is not created because he had a strong mother and a weak father, but because the only tenderness he ever had was with the father, a member of the same sex.

Dr. Fink said the female homosexual often didn't have a father who was accepting and so turned back to her mother, then to other females, for love.

Homosexuality with this firm a base is not likely to change in later life, he said, although homosexuality that is essentially a defence built up out of simple fear of the opposite sex may be treated.

Clipping: "Gay San Francisco,"
Weekend Magazine, *July 1979*

A homosexual who tries to hide the nature of his sexuality is said to be in the closet. Should he abandon the attempt to hide he will be said to have come out. Homosexuals are now coming out in great numbers, and as though in imitation of a law of nature many heterosexuals are manifesting an equal but opposite reaction.

"If society is to allow and promote homosexuality," wrote Staff Sergeant Thomas Moclair in a recent issue of the Toronto police union's monthly newsletter, "then why not other acts? Why not condone murder, assault and rape? Those people are sick in the head, too."

Handwritten notes on white paper

Sometimes I think I must be out of my mind. Here I am—
in early middle age, well established in my profession, well
known and regarded in my community, married to a very
intelligent, talented, charming woman who is a first-class
mother to our wonderful children. All this may very well be
put into jeopardy by this incredible sexual adventure which I
have embarked on. But have I any choice? No. I don't think so.

Journal entry on lined paper

31.1.80

Last night, I made it with a Roman Catholic priest. When I
turned around and our eyes met at Buddy's, he looked like
anything but a priest. With long blond hair curled tightly
against his head, and a sexy, textured white shirt open halfway
to his waist, very masculine and with a fresh tan which he had
got in Key West, Al was one of the more gorgeous-looking
men in the bar.

He introduced himself first as a university professor in
psychology at D__, where in fact he teaches part-time. It
wasn't until later in the evening that I discovered he is also a
priest at a prestigious parish in B__. I could then see a glimpse
of that quiet confidence which so often marks a cleric, but, as
I was soon to find out, it was combined with an astonishing
need to have his attractiveness and good body reaffirmed.

He kept asking me to tell him what I liked about him,
what it was about him that attracted me to him in the bar.
When we first met, he told me I was a handsome man, which
was a nice surprise, but later when we talked about it, he
admitted how much he needed compliments on his own attractiveness. He thinks this is in part due to the fact that his
mother is Portuguese, all the rest of the family is dark and
he was the ugly duckling, in his mother's eyes at least. But
he supports the theory that physical beauty can be a burden
when this almost inevitably becomes an important aspect of
the person and his definition of himself.

Al graduated from university at about 19, went into the priesthood and led an incredibly disciplined life until his late thirties. Somewhere along the way, he also picked up a doctorate of psychology. He claims that he didn't even masturbate from the time he entered the priesthood until he was 33. He didn't smoke or drink alcohol, tea or coffee and owned two black suits. Then, he came out, abandoned his collar and acquired a vast wardrobe of smart clothes.

Al struck me as being remarkably at ease with being a gay parish priest—in fact, he talked about giving up teaching in order to devote more time to his parish. He clearly enjoys letting people realize that not all priests are dour, sober characters. He talked about coming back on the plane from Key West with a woman in her fifties who kept saying over her Bloody Marys, "I can't believe you are a priest!" I can imagine that, in fact, he would be beautifully relaxed, friendly and genial with his parishioners, but can he really keep his gay identity separate?

His bishop knows that he is gay and told him he could have gay friends, but no genital contact. He certainly was not following the bishop's instructions last night. Al has quite a circle of friends with whom he keeps in touch and comes to Toronto once a month for his diet of gay life. He says he doesn't think he would ever like to live with another person so perhaps he is coming to terms with his profession and gayness. Although he said that he, like me, had trouble concentrating on intellectual matters ever since he came out.

I asked him what had led to his coming out. He said he had been very ill and almost died with two perforated ulcers. His doctor was amazed that he had been able apparently to suppress the pain so that he wasn't even aware of it and he thinks that it was all related to his suppressing his homosexuality as well. In any case, that day he came home from the hospital, everything looked beautiful, life was exciting and he decided on the spur of the moment to go to New York, where he met a man coming out of a play, was seduced and has been gay ever since. That was three years ago.

Excerpts from Twelfth Night *by William Shakespeare,*
handwritten on lined paper

If music be the food of love, play on;
Give me excess of it, that, surfeiting,
The appetite may sicken, and so die. (I,i)

What is love? 'tis not hereafter;
Present mirth hath present laughter;
What's to come is still unsure;
In delay there lies no plenty (II,iii)

For such as I am all true lovers are,
Unstaid and skittish in all motions else,
Save in the constant image of the creature
That is beloved. (II,iv)

A murderous guilt shows not itself more soon
Than love that would seem hid: love; night is noon (III,i)

What relish is in this? How runneth the stream?
Or I am mad or else this is a dream:
Let fancy still my sense in Lethe steep;
If it be thus to dream, still let me sleep! (IV,ii)

Fate, show thy force: ourselves we do not owe;
What is decreed must be, and be this so. (I,v)

Journal entries on lined notepad

23.3.80

Meeting Tom has been one of the most wonderful things
that has happened to me—but also, inevitably, profoundly
disturbing.

After his PhD at London School of Economics Tom
had been a film director making documentaries for the BBC.
For the last five years he had been teaching in the Graduate
School of Design at Harvard. But, above all, he was bright,
intelligent, witty, and I felt an instantaneous meeting of
minds. Obviously he did too. He said we had to spend the
night together; I agreed. As we walked to the flat where he
was staying, he said he liked me because I was a real person
and that he knew we were going to be friends for a long time.
Normally that sort of hasty concluding makes me suspicious
and wary, but in this case I loved it. We often have our best
times when things go dreadfully wrong and we certainly
started that way.

When we got back to the supposedly empty apartment,
we found a stranger already in bed. He got up; we proceeded
to make embarrassed introductions. He was an artist who
was also a friend of the man whose apartment it was. Tom
handled the situation beautifully. He admired the man's
pictures and after chatting for a while, announced, "Joe and I
are gay and you're not and we are planning to spend the night
together, so you go back to bed and we'll stay in the living
room." The man was very kind, however, and offered his bed.

By this time, I knew that I liked Tom a lot simply as someone who was great fun to be with. . . .

I had planned to go back to Peterborough the next day, but Tom wanted to go dancing and I said I would be delighted. Later in the afternoon I met him at his office and heard more about the work he was doing. He was on leave from Harvard to make a film with the group who had made such an impact with the *Connections* documentary on the mafia a few years ago.

Almost every time we are together, we talk a lot and laugh a lot. Tom has remarked on various occasions how we "click," how there is a "zing," how we understand each other's so-often literary or intellectual humour. And last Thursday at our picnic with Flip, Flip said the same thing—"You guys are always laughing."

Tom had to go back to Boston. He thought it might be for a couple of weeks and that was my first experience in seeing days stretch into weeks. I also became increasingly desperate as I realized that my sabbatical was slipping away. An election had been called for 18 February and I realized I wouldn't be able to leave Canada until at least the beginning of March. I knew I still had a lot to do, but was terribly bored with the book* and fed up with living in Ptbo. The book was proceeding at a snail's pace and that just increased my sense of panic. I thought of moving to Toronto—at least there, I would be able to mix work and pleasure.

---

* a history of the Liberal Party of Canada

Finally on 5 February, Tom was back in town. I met him at his office—a wonderful moment, though, oddly, slightly different from how I had remembered him. We went to the Chinese restaurant in the basement on Dundas. Tom clearly had had a bad day. The financing of the film was shaky and, to top that off, a medical exam had discovered that he was mildly diabetic. But he loved the restaurant—we share a fascination for cheap, sleazy restaurants that serve good food—and then we went out for a drink at Neighbour's. But Tom was distracted by his worries and suddenly announced that he wanted to go back to Ian's and call Bob, his lover in Boston. I was so disappointed, and bitterly reminded of the fact that he was already committed.

On the Saturday afternoon of the weekend we first met, Tom had told me a lot about Bob, but Tom was afraid that already the end was inevitable. Tom wanted a monogamous relationship, but Bob had a need to be admired and sought after and Bob was drinking heavily. My reaction was to think that perhaps Tom was freer than he had first suggested, but, at the same time, I felt for him and admired him tremendously for his sense of loyalty.

But now, with Tom leaving me to call Bob, he had dashed my hopes for him. I sought out E at Katrina's and, for the second time in a month, I wept sadly on his shoulder. I told him I wondered if I really was suited for the gay world, to which he replied that I made a very good faggot because I cried so beautifully. I rather liked that!

The next day, Tom called me, obviously in much better

spirits, asked if we were getting together that evening, and I said only if he really wanted to. He got the message and said, yes, he would like to. We went to the play *Something Red* that Richard Monette was in. I had already seen it once before, but was interested to see if it would be as good the second time without the surprise of the Russian roulette. I also wanted to see if Tom and I shared the same taste in theatre. We did. But the most wonderful thing about that evening was that he came back with me to my room at Hart House. . . .

During the next three months, I went home each weekend, usually meeting Paul on Saturday afternoon for a dim sum lunch and driving him back to St. Andrew's* on Sunday evening. Sunday afternoon, I took Flip skiing at Devil's Elbow and while he went downhill, I did the cross-country track. Alone with my thoughts, I recalled what Tom and I had done the previous week, what he had said, and was struck by how much I missed him. In Toronto, just being with him gave me such a sense of elation, but I took it all in stride, the many laughs we had, our shared interests and the deeply satisfying sex. But each weekend back in Peterborough, I realized more and more how much I missed him and how much I was falling in love with him. Each week in Toronto, our relationship acquired a new depth.

The next week, Tom and I didn't do anything like going to a film, but after dinner, he came back to Hart House with

---

* St. Andrew's College, where my brother Paul did one (unhappy) year of high school me. One night, when we came in, he took off his trousers, asked me to pour him a drink and said how relaxed he felt with me. And we *were* wonderfully relaxed together. We talked and drank and talked and, one night, I played a tape of the Love Duet from *Tristan und Isolde*, which he did not know, and we made love to some of the most beautiful music I know.

I think it was on the Saturday morning that the word *love* first passed between us. (Thankfully, so unlike the other silly men who say they love you half an hour after you have started kissing!) We had often talked about the incredible understanding we had for each other and how we both knew how much we liked each other. But this time, Tom said that we were starting to fall in love with each other and did we realize the consequences, especially as both of us already had commitments. By this time, I had already started to ponder what Tom might mean to my life and to realize that ours was such an exceptional relationship, that *he* was so exceptional, that I felt prepared to accept the consequences of our being in love.

I like Anne a lot and feel a strong sense of duty towards her and the kids, but more and more, especially after being in Toronto, I realize that I simply can't live at home in Ptbo week in and week out, even if there were no Tom. Miraculously, Anne has not complained about my time away from Ptbo and perhaps that will make possible a loose kind of *modus vivendi*.

As for Tom, here was the physical affection, the intelligence, the artistic sensitivity, a comparable career and, not least, the sheer sexual fulfillment which I had so longed for. Yes, I could accept the consequences.

That morning, a light snow (the first for weeks) was falling as we left the side door of Hart House together. Tom looked at me with such love in his eyes and said he wanted to kiss me. It was public and he couldn't, but I knew how far we had come.

March 5 began the wonderful month when we lived together in BW's apartment in Toronto. Tom had got the apartment and invited me to share it with him. It was a very comfortable, stylishly furnished apartment with that unmistakable stamp of faggot money about it.

It is difficult to put into words the utter joy I felt in actually living with Tom. Everything had an excitement about it—making shopping lists and going to all the various shops in the area—almost like shopping in France, playing BW's records, sharing the same gigantic bath towel and especially those tête-à-tête dinners and the conversations that stretched on until Tom announced that we were going to bed. . . .

The most spectacular night, probably, was the time we had a dinner party for Bob and Ben. I had, at long last, finished my book and that afternoon had indexed the chart, tables, table of contents, preface—everything. Bob and Ben were great fun and we even came up with a title for my book—Bob had yawned and made fun of *Inside the Liberal Party* and I had challenged them all to come up with something better. When Tom suggested *The L-Shaped Party*—we all agreed that was it. But by that time, I had had a great deal to drink and scribbled down the title for fear of forgetting it (next morning, I did).

One evening that week, Anne and Alison came for a quick dinner after a doctor's appointment for Alison. I was nervous about it—would they inspect the sleeping arrangements?—but very much wanted to bring these two parts of my life together—to continue to have Anne become gradually aware of what I was doing. They had a great time together—Alison wanted Tom to see us in the summer. Tom and Anne joked about my cooking messes in the kitchen.

That weekend was the one when I took Paul and Flip skiing for four days. Flip is always lively and amusing (a bit "off the wall," as Tom would say). There was a period when Paul and I never had very much to talk about, but in the last year, he has become interested in politics and I enjoy giving him little mini-lectures, when, for instance, he asks me about the American primaries. The skiing was mixed and Tom was never far from my thoughts . . .

Wednesday, I wanted to cook a special dinner for Tom. I got fresh asparagus, pheasant and strawberries to go with Tom's honey melon. I also had a special 1971 claret from the purchase I had made several years ago. The meal went wonderfully well (asparagus was perfect) and afterwards, Tom told me how much he appreciated my sense of occasion. He was obviously very moved. We played *La Bohème* and after I had sat with my eyes closed for a long time, he reached across the table to take my hands and we looked into each other's eyes. Never have I felt so deeply in love nor so deeply loved.

*Excerpt from a draft of an unfinished letter from
my father, handwritten on blue airmail paper*

Munich, 23.4.80

Dear Tom,

. . . My life all seems to be such a hopeless tangle—
though I agree with Daniel Martin* that it is hard to have
sympathy for one who has such an inordinate share of the
world's riches—both material and, at least to outside ob-
servers, emotional—though you know some of the reality
of the latter. I *had* hoped that one of the insights of this trip
might be a clearer idea of where I am going. That may, by
some miracle, still come. But so far, it has served only to
reinforce my feelings about you—how much I simply enjoy
being with you—which, somehow, in Toronto I can take in
stride, but which, here, is more difficult to cope with. . . .

I am sitting on the edge of a vast German beer hall,
while a Bavarian band plays "Roll Out the Barrel" and
German Fraüleins laugh hysterically—oh, world!

As far as Anne and the kids are concerned, the
3,000-mile perspective has changed very little there
either—so far. They *have* to know that I am not your
standard Daddy/husband—and I hope to hell to keep
their respect and love in this gradual unveiling process,
but I know that I can't and don't want to keep up the
pretence of the last 15+ years. I think, ultimately, it is up
to them to decide what they can accept.

---

* the eponymous protagonist in the novel by John Fowles

On every count (i.e., not *just* Anne and the kids), I know I have to have patience if I am going to achieve any kind of solution, but that has been and remains difficult. I think back to that evening in Wagstaff's apartment when you played some Elgar and I became very nostalgic and commented that, after all, perhaps each of us is really alone—and that seems to be one of the few things that doesn't get easier to bear as we get older. I also have this perhaps naive faith that we don't have to be quite as alone as we so often force ourselves to be—though one might think that by 43 I should know better.

I hope you won't think me unkind if I say that you are more worldly experienced than I (the Daniel Martin side) and I may simply be naive when I say that two souls rarely touch, as ours have, in one's lifetime. At the very least, our friendship or whatever it is has helped me enormously in wanting to make Anne and the kids aware of my minority sexual orientation—I will always be grateful to you for that dinner with Alison and Anne and the picnic with Flip because I see these occasions as a few hesitant initial steps of the sort which I shall have to take further if I am going to bring my life once again into some kind of harmonious whole, if indeed this is possible.

Beyond that, if I am right about our mutuality (and time could still prove me/us wrong), I would hope that somehow, sometime, we could seize the opportunity provided. In the meantime, I think it means also that each of us has a rather awesome responsibility to the other—and not, in some misguided way, to be *kind*, but to be *honest*. So I thank you for your honesty.

This has been *heavy* and not too easy to write, but has helped me to get back to some sort of equilibrium.

Handwritten notes on airmail paper

Munich, 23.4.80

. . . . Anne is a person whom I like and respect enormously and she has shared more of my life experiences than anyone. . . . she can't be kept in the dark any
longer. . . . I haven't had any mail from her, in spite of
regular letters from this end and a couple of telephone
calls. She has never been a great letter writer, but I find
this ominous.

For me, life is very much about close personal relationships and I know I have been neglecting these while
chasing will-o'-the-wisps in Toronto. I want to take some
time with those close personal relationships this summer
and I suppose it will be revealing to see the reaction to
my "story."

White pages, manual typewriter: "My Story," written
at the suggestion of the Gay Fathers support group

Today, I want to write "My Story," because it seems I know
where I'm at. Tomorrow, I may be less certain; yesterday I was
quite confused. In reality I am probably not quite as much at
cross-purposes as my introduction would indicate, because I
know that, even in the face of dramatic changes externally,
there are still many constants in one's life.

The public facts are that I am married to an intelligent,
attractive, personable woman; we have three lovely children,
a comfortable house in a spacious residential section of the
small city where we live; I am successful in my profession;
both my wife and I are active and well-known in various community organizations; and two years ago, I acknowledged,
finally, that I was a homosexual.

That aspect of my story has much in common with the
stories of so many other men—the teenage friendships in
which the element of sexual infatuation was kept severely
in check and tightly closeted, the terror of the tell-tale
erection in changing rooms and swimming pools, and
the horror of admitting, even to myself, that I might be
"queer." I wanted to be like my peers, playing team sports
(which I secretly hated) and dating girls (which I certainly
preferred to team sports). My talents and achievements,
however, were much more considerable in the area of
intellectual and artistic endeavours. I can remember being
teased about not filling masculine prescriptions very well,

but that made me only more determined to succumb to all the pressures to conform.

Similar conforming pressures also came from the moral-religious precepts of my parents and family. I grew up in a happy, upper-middle-class environment, where there was always lots of talking, arguing, laughing and, occasionally, some emotion and tears. My father, especially, was a stalwart churchman. He certainly preached Victorian sexual morality and, I assume, practised it. I accepted all this without difficulty—with conviction, in fact, because I saw the family of my childhood as a happy proof of the rightness of these ideals.

As I came into my mid-teens, I started to date girls, just as all my friends did, and I hoped that I would eventually be the father in a family like the one I grew up in. I have always liked female company, perhaps because, after my father died, I felt closest to the female members of my family.

At university, I apparently acquired a certain reputation for playing the field (I was teased again about that just a short time ago); but I preferred to date girls who were lots of fun and didn't put me under any sexual pressure. Sometimes, I worried about not "knowing how" to neck and I remember one painful double-date, which my friend and mentor recommended as essential to my education. After a movie, we parked in a secluded spot. The sounds from the back seat indicated that my friend was using his considerable charm and skills to good effect; in the front seat, my date and I both sat nervously, while I attempted to go through the motions which my friend had told me to make. It was with immense relief that we finally terminated the evening and I didn't try that sort of thing again for a long time. Of course, I could draw comfort from the fact that I was abiding by the precepts of my Victorian upbringing and avoiding the possible disasters of premarital sex about which I had been warned. What I only dimly realized then was that these principles of sexual morality were endangered far more by the emotions which my male friends aroused in me. It was easy to be a good boy as far as girls were concerned.

It wasn't until graduate school that I began to consider that homosexuality might be anything other than an utterly distasteful, immoral lifestyle. I fell completely in love with a fellow student who was my closest friend through graduate school. We travelled together, eventually lived together, and always talked endlessly. We even discussed homosexuality, but he believed the theory that homosexuality was something one grew out of.

I still thought homosexuality was morally wrong, although there were certainly times when I would have surrendered with relief to the consuming sexual longing which I felt for my friend. We came very close to doing something about this attraction, which, I think, was mutual; but one or the other always held back. Also, a number of women shared the passion I felt for my undoubtedly attractive friend and I suspect—we have never discussed it frankly—that he may have been an example himself of someone who did grow into heterosexuality. Undoubtedly there was also a certain causal link between this and my coming back to the notion, finally, that a Christian marriage, after all, was best. The brain had won the day—even if other parts of the body felt differently.

By this time, I admitted to myself that I had homosexual "tendencies," but I believed that self-discipline could successfully overcome them. I had worked hard to achieve other things—why not that as well? Besides, I convinced myself that, because I had never actually had a homosexual *experience*, I was not really a homosexual and would outgrow these "tendencies" anyway.

I read two novels which made a profound impression on me: *Advise and Consent* and *Brideshead Revisited.* The first was recommended by a tutor as one of the best insights into how the Congressional system in Washington really worked. One of the main characters, Senator Brigham Anderson, was homosexual and that was exciting, but when the truth about his past was about to come out, he committed suicide. That was a blunt, horrific warning. The first part of *Brideshead* takes place at Oxford and the two main characters, Charles and Sebastian, have what may be a homosexual relationship. But it fizzles out and the principal character outgrows his homosexual infatuation and goes on to fall in love with his boyfriend's sister. That confirmed the theory that homosexual attraction was merely a stage in the maturing process that one grew out of, just as the boys at English boarding schools went on to normal heterosexual relationships after they left school.

Fortunately, I had met an attractive, highly intelligent, talented woman for whom I had very warm feelings of affection (and still do) and, after a punctiliously correct Victorian courtship, we were married. She is the only woman I have ever really wanted to marry—not that I felt a powerful sexual attraction, but at least the idea of sex was not repellent, which frankly was the case with virtually all the others.

Things did not go badly at first. I was captivated with the *idea* of the marriage bed, though I remember wondering, with apprehension, if one was expected to go through this sort of thing *every* night. In our case, one wasn't. For a number of years, illness, pregnancy and childbirth effectively eliminated sex for months at a time. After that, sex became occasional. Even simple physical contact never became a significant part of our marriage and I often found her in the morning asleep in another room. I missed physical contact desperately and felt rejected and angry at times, but found, eventually, that I could accept the situation stoically.

Sex became occasional and perfunctory, even anxious, and I have to admit that I was just as often relieved to be turned down. We joked about sex, but didn't really discuss it, and in spite of everything, we became closer over the years simply as two people who lived together and achieved a kind of unspoken *modus vivendi*, even a warm comradeship which arose from many shared interests—our children, house, friends, and various artistic pursuits. In our social lives, we have never been dependent on each other; we go our separate ways as often as we do things together.

I don't remember when my homosexual "tendencies" revived or whether they ever disappeared completely, except that within a few years of being married I can remember deluding myself into thinking that I could admire certain men in a platonic way and even harbour secret fantasies of being seduced. For many years, I felt that I had achieved a kind of sexual equilibrium—I was aware of being physically attracted to various men who often became good friends.

Music, too, was a terribly important outlet. I think I am probably a reasonably self-disciplined person; but certainly at heart I am very romantic and for years my most sensual experiences came from the music of Chopin, Brahms, Wagner, Verdi, Elgar.

Gradually, though, I came to realize that I had to experience physical male love. Looking back over the years since I was a teenager, I realize that one of the constants in my life has been the necessity of having at least one male friend who excited me intellectually, emotionally and physically. (Those friendships are mostly still important. The object of my early teen infatuation still raises those nice warm feelings, though I may see him only once a year.) Through all those friendships, though, I was always frustrated at being unable to act out the physical attraction.

As I went into my mid-thirties, I more and more consciously began looking for a new friend, except that this time, he would be homosexual and would seduce me! At age 39, I thought I had found him. A somewhat younger man moved to town. I heard some promising gossip about him. I introduced myself and soon we became close friends. It was like another high school romance. He telephoned me every day and we saw each other constantly. He even mentioned being friends with a notoriously gay man in his profession—and then announced that he was going to be married. The same old story all over again!

That experience, however, made me realize how desperately I wanted a gay friendship and that romance might still be possible at the ripe age of 39. So, I decided that if I couldn't find a gay friendship *within* my closet, then I would have to try looking *outside*. But the alternative of walking into a gay establishment in Toronto terrified me. What if I met someone I knew?

Then several things happened. First, I turned forty and decided I would soon be too old to try the gay option, if I didn't now. Second, I read a newspaper article about a gay father, a professional man of about my age, and the first openly homosexual man with whom I could identify. Third, I attended a conference at the other end of the country where I was sure that I could go into a gay bar without meeting anyone I knew. But I did—the man in the newspaper article! I poured out my story and, for the first time, revealed my innermost secrets to another human being. I remember telling him that I *had* to find out if I was gay, but that it really would be much simpler if I discovered I wasn't. Well, I did and I was. In fact, I was amazed at how *natural*—yes, *natural*—it all felt and how uninhibited I was. So much for Victorian prudery! And instead of the feelings of great guilt which I was sure I would feel afterwards, it was as if a great weight had been lifted off me. At last I knew who I was.

For a period after that, I was ravenous, like a man who has just escaped from a prison diet of bread and water. I did things, like going to the baths, which I had thought quite out of keeping with my character. But gradually I came to realize that I am still the same person I have always been. I still like Brahms better than disco; I still admire a fine mind as much as a fine body. Indeed, now I can be myself with even fewer self-imposed constraints than before. (My straight friends, I know, would add that my behaviour has always been marked by a certain lack of inhibition.)

Coming out has been a fascinating experience. The tremendous understanding and affection of gay friends, the chance encounters (whether sexual or not) with interesting, attractive men, the highly developed gay community structures—these are features of gay life which were unexpected and make me glad to be gay. And even the sudden realization that I am now a member of a misunderstood, harassed minority group has had the benefit of reawakening my sensitivity to issues of individual rights and freedoms. I still have trouble coping with what seems to be the roller coaster of gay life. My own emotions rise and fall with startling intensity, and so often after a pleasant brief exchange with someone, both of you are soon gone in opposite directions.

Where am I now? My home life has been remarkably placid. I come and go as I feel I must and answer truthfully (if briefly) the few questions that are raised. My wife may or may not know. I have adopted the strategy of trying to make my family gradually aware that daddy is gay. At times, I long to tell my wife everything, but fear that conversation might be our last. As long as my home life continues peacefully, it seems unwise to provoke a dramatic change.

I know, also, that I need regularly to have gay sex, to relax in a gay environment, and to be able to participate in gay social causes. Most of all, I need one or more close friends, like those I have had over the years, except that now we can allow our love to manifest itself in physical ways. I guess, after all, that there is a common thread to my story since that is what I said to my graduate school friend in an unguarded moment almost twenty years ago.

But it didn't happen then and often seems as difficult to achieve now. Then, there was friendship and no sex. Now the sex is easy, but combining it with friendship is the difficult part, because the gay world seems to be rigidly divided into mutually exclusive categories: friends who do not have sex together; one-night stands between men who have no intention of getting to know each other; and all-consuming lovers.

To pursue the goal of sexual gay friendship, while maintaining a heterosexual marriage without sex, makes the squaring of a circle look like child's play by comparison. I confess to periodic bouts of melancholia over the prospects.

I dread the possibility that I may lose my wife and family in exchange for an endless, cheerless round of bars and baths. Still, I have to face the fact that I cannot love my wife as a man should be able to love his wife, but I believe that I can love a man as some men love other men. My fantasy is ultimately to love and live with a man of similar age, interests and education (how bourgeois!) without having destroyed the bonds of affection which I feel for my wife and children, nor their respect for me. Perhaps, really, we are all like Camus' doctor in *The Plague*—doing what we feel we must do, what is right for us, and not worrying too much about whether it is really possible or not. . . .

For two brief months I had the sort of relationship that I had always longed for. While doing some work in Toronto, I met a man who was also working there for a time. From the moment we met, we both felt an instantaneous rapport—same profession, many shared interests, common acquaintances, some amazing coincidences in our respective careers—even to both growing up in two different cities on streets with the same name. And we had a very similar sense of the ridiculous, which we discovered on the occasion of our first night together—an almost impossible situation, which we both relished for its zany madness.

It wasn't long before we were living together. We were both working hard in our jobs and I was more productive than I had been for months. Our evening recreation was simple, usually a meal together and talk, but what wonderful, intimate talk it was. We talked a lot about our pasts—the pleasures, the frustrations, the hurts. My friend has been gay all his adult life and in this respect our two lives have been very different. To me he seemed much more sophisticated, much better able to deal with the vagaries of gay life than I; but I learned that we nevertheless shared many of the same vulnerabilities and I loved him the more for that. This communion, intertwined with the physical and sexual, allowed me to experience for the first time in my life the intimacy which I had always imagined to be part of marriage; but I had found it at last with another man.

We largely avoided talking about the future. I think we both probably started off thinking that this would be a pleasant affair for two men away from home, although the first night we met, my friend said he knew we were both going to be an important part of each other's lives for a long time. Soon we were each making chance remarks which revealed we were falling in love. But I was due to leave the country for a few months. Besides, I was married, my friend was still involved in a rocky relationship with a man in his home city, and, within a few months, we would both be living and working 400 miles apart. On the two brief occasions when we allowed the future to cast its shadow on present laughter, I said I was prepared to accept the consequences of our love, but my friend, having asked the question, warned about making assumptions for the future.

In our last few days together, we were closer than ever. I left for my trip abroad with great apprehensions, but consoled myself with the thought that if our love could not survive a two-month absence, then it was not the sort of relationship I wanted anyway.

Life is a continuum. None of our stories will have an end until the day we die. Certainly I cannot now come to any conclusions about mine. On returning home from my trip,

I realized even more how much I was in love. I had missed my friend dreadfully, but he was no longer anxious to continue the relationship as it had been before. He had suffered some traumatic changes in his own life, and whether his new coolness towards me was a temporary phase or a permanent change, I could not tell for certain, though I feared the worst. I became very depressed and confused. This relationship that had seemed so special just a few months before—had it been, really, only a passing affair? Was this an aspect of gay life that one had to toughen oneself for?—like the impersonal, detached, fast sex of the baths—except that it lasts a bit longer? But I don't want to be tough and cast off lovers like last season's trendy trousers.

I still desperately want that lasting, intimate relationship with a man of similar interests, age and education, but I have become intensely weary of the typically gay hunt, the seemingly endless visual examination and pursuit of men with whom one finds subsequently one had virtually nothing in common—though it is perhaps some consolation that this abortive discovery is frequently postponed until the breakfast table. In any case, I strongly suspect that the sort of men I want to meet have given up long ago on the classic gay introduction grounds. Indeed they are probably happily at home with their lovers, which is even more disturbing. But I am also afraid of getting so involved again, knowing the pain that came after just two short months. My friend used to talk about his scar tissue, and I wonder if there is something self-destructive about gay life which threatens to make emotional cripples of so many of us. Are gay men their own worst enemies?

My friend says he sees us now as being "very good friends." Except for the occasional short kiss that doesn't seem to be very much of an improvement on those platonic adolescent friendships of twenty-five years ago. On the home front, I have attempted to keep my tears to myself, though I suspect my wife has deduced much of what has taken place in my love life, and we avoid talking about what is important— not much progress there either.

First of all, I want to thank you very much for helping out Anne when she got in touch with you last month. I know it came as a shock to you to hear that your brother is homosexual, but I think she was right to go to you.

I had a letter from Anne's lawyer last week that brought everything out in the open and was really a great relief for both of us. Anne has been incredibly calm and understanding. I always knew she was a wonderful person, but never more than now. We are proceeding with a separation agreement and are looking at the possibility of my staying here three nights a week in the hope that this will give me continuing contact with her and the kids—something we both want. Please be assured that I have never had any intention of running out on my obligations here as, I guess, Anne feared when she first learned of my other attachments.

My life has been very disoriented and difficult over the last two years or more and especially the last few months. I really don't expect you to agree with what I have done, but I'm sure you must wonder why this has happened to a member of your family. Maybe it will help a bit if you read the attached "story." I wrote it for a support group I am in. In it, I tried to look back over my life as honestly as I could and simply set down how it is that I am where I am. I found it all very painful, but the experience was probably good therapy. Maybe it will help you at least to understand, but maybe not.

I have been very worried about what I was going to say to Dot. Anne says you have already spoken to her. I would rather have decided myself how to tackle that one—but I would like to know whether you have discussed it with her.

I am genuinely sorry for all the distress I am causing everyone—including myself. Because of the disappointments over the last few months, which you can read about in my "story," I wonder if this "gay life" isn't a dead end for me. I often wish there was such a thing as a "straight" pill—I would have attempted to swallow the whole bottle. Still, I guess we all have to accept who we are and what we are and hope that the people we love can do the same. I do hope very much that your harsh judgement of me can be softened as time goes by. If it were not for Anne and a few close friends who have stood by me and consoled me, I'm sure I would feel very desperate.

Handwritten draft of a letter from my father to Char Crane,
one of his oldest friends, and her husband, 1980

Christmas Eve—
Dear Char and Graham—

I have been late sending my Christmas greetings to
you because I was not sure how to phrase them. I could
start by saying that I feel a whole lot better about the world
and my life in it than when I saw you early last summer.

I have never felt as desperate or dejected as I did
then and that's why I went to see you. We are such old
friends and I had always felt that no matter what the
problem was, I could discuss it with you both. In fact,
do you remember, Char, that years ago—I'm not sure
when—you assured me that I could always count on you
in that way?

Our meeting last spring was a pretty emotional
one—not surprisingly, I suppose. I was hurt by some of
the things you said and you were upset by what I had to
relate. Six months have passed since then and neither of
us has got in touch with the other. Have you wondered
how I have been getting along? I guess I have learned
that ultimately one has to rely on oneself to tackle life's
problems and mysteries and to be thankful that, even
in times of the blackest despair, one finds, somewhere
within, resources to draw on, to come out and face the
day again with confidence and joy in being alive and
being oneself.

As I think about where I am now and where I go from here, I keep coming back to three very basic facts about myself—I am a husband, I am a father and I am a homosexual. The last named is the attribute of longest standing, though it is also the one which I have had the greatest difficulty in accepting. Perhaps if I had been more honest with myself twenty or twenty-five years ago, I would not now be attempting to reconcile the apparently conflicting responsibilities that flow from each. On the other hand, I would not have known the love of four people who are all so tremendously important to me now.

Sometimes I wonder why all of this has happened to me, but I know there is no point in speculating about hypothetical pasts, only about where to go from here. I would like to be a good husband, a good father and a good homosexual. It would be a lot easier to be the first two without being the third and there have been times when I have longed for some magical pill or drastic operation that would relieve me of the necessity of attempting to be a good homosexual. But even assuming it was possible, I know that I would be copping out on other homosexuals, especially homosexual fathers. We all have to deal with rejection and misunderstanding by family and friends, but the more that each of us fights his own battles against prejudices, the less torment there should be for those who come after us.

My brother has told his son that my parents would roll over in their graves if they knew about me. We can

each draw whatever inspiration we wish from the memories of our parents. I prefer to remember my father as
a man whose politics were very much motivated by the
concern he felt for the underprivileged of this world—
both he and my mother having experienced considerable
hardship in their pasts. Their children have not known
economic hardship, but one of them now knows about
intolerance and injustice first-hand. I would not expect my
parents to have made my cause their cause, but I would
like to think that they could understand why I must accept
the challenge which lies before all gay people today.

I don't want to be ashamed of being gay; I don't
want my wife to be ashamed of being married to a gay
man and I don't want my children to be ashamed of
having a gay father. It will be a long slow process, but I
know that this is the only way in which I can find peace
within myself.

As I sat in church this afternoon pondering the
ancient message of Christmas, I realized that I did want
to write to you in the spirit of love and charity and to say
that I still want your help and friendship. And even if you
can never quite accept what I am, perhaps it will be that
much easier when, in the future, someone else whom you
love tells you that he or she is homosexual and asks for
your help and understanding.

Thank you very much for the help you have given
Anne. Even if in different ways, she needs support as
much as I do.

Endnote

The Christmas Eve letter was the final document in The Box. My father stopped keeping a journal; once his story had been told, he no longer felt the need. The Box sat in my father's office for a decade, was eventually moved to the basement, and it remained unopened for more than thirty years.

Four months after he wrote the Christmas Eve letter, my father met Lance, his partner of thirty-one years. And counting.

PART THREE

The Way She Saw It

A Marriage Requiem

1. *Kyrie*

At age twenty-nine, I went to live with my mother.

It had been twelve years since I'd fled Peterborough and I had spent the time riding inspirations and whims around the world. Trudging homeward only for occasional visits, I would feel a haughty curl forming on my lip the moment I veered off the highway onto familiar ground. I had spent years quietly despising the place and my history there, unaware that until we make peace with our homes, we can never quite make peace with ourselves.

After spinning across continents, through innumerable borders and languages, what finally propelled me back home was nothing more exotic than heartbreak, that sensation of a quilled wreckage in my body. By the time I returned to "mend my heart for a while," my mother was living on a farm several miles out of town to which she and Mel had moved and where he had died of a sickness in his bones.

And so my mother was newly widowed after thirteen years of marriage; I, freshly severed from love. It was a beautiful pairing at an unusual time of life, and we were a good match for each other. The first night we sat out under a shatter of stars, back to back, holding each other up as we talked.

As a young girl, I had suffered asthma, a self-suffocation that is difficult to describe—more difficult still to endure. If it got serious when my mother was out, I would curl up on the floor and prop myself up with pillows, wheezing and gasping until she got home. While my dad was there, sympathetic and caring, hers was the comfort that allowed me to relax enough that the air could find me. The same was true at twenty-nine, with a constricted heart instead of lungs.

My mom lived with two greyhounds, both rescued from southern racetracks, their faces and bodies pulled into the permanent shape of wind. There were also two blind and bedraggled Bichon Frisés, and I added to the household a cat I'd found the day my heart became imprinted with the tread of my lover's indifferent shoe.

I had been emptying myself of our common-law marriage, raggedly packing the last of my boxes into my car, when I heard a kitten squeaking in the alley. It was alone, a creature smaller than my hand, eyes blossoming with pus—dead if I did not pick it up. I tucked it into my coat pocket, put the final few boxes in the car, and blew a kiss to my old life. Then I sped to a friend's house, where I spent the evening sobbing and drizzling drops of camomile across the kitten's swollen eyes. It was so fragile, I remember thinking as I sat in that chilled hollow Montreal kitchen, that I could easily have closed its throat with my thumb. That night the kitten slept on my pillow, rooting through my hair, its thimble lips desperate to suckle my scalp and the quiet cove behind my ears. If anything got me through that first pain-soaked, lonely night, it was that begging of one life for another.

At dawn, I put the kitten in a box and pulled out of town, leaving trailings of myself along the streets and neighbourhoods that had become—briefly—my home. On the highway back to Ontario, I let my foot fall heavy, imagining the ease with which I could twitch myself into oncoming traffic and leave my heart scattered on the road. When I arrived at my mother's farm, I got out of the car and lay down fully clothed in the creek next to the house. As I pressed into its pebble-bed cradle, feeling liquid winter purling against my ears and a cold so intense it pounded through my bones, I asked the water to find mercy enough to swallow me.

Then came my mother's voice, calling out from the cedar twig bridge that arched over the water: "Wouldn't you prefer a warm bath?" She was smiling with the kitten rescued from the car and tucked into the front of her jacket, his opal eyes blinking out tentatively. The three of us taking in the peculiar shape of our new lives.

II. *Dies Irae*

In the years since her second marriage, my mother and I had been both distant and close, caring for each other from opposite ends of the globe, through letters and family occasions. We had never really talked about my father except in practical terms—*Christmas Day is with Dad this year, so we'll see you on Boxing Day*—and aside from one laughter-filled backpacking trip through Sicily together when I was twenty-one, my mother and I had never had time on our own to pull ourselves back through family history and sort it all out.

Until time was all we had. And a farm. Some animals to care for. Silence. And two raw hearts swollen with pain.

"When everything started falling apart during the divorce, I remember thinking I was never going to get over it," my mom said one night by the fireplace, a scratchy mohair blanket tucked in around her legs and my little alley-kitten, Figleaf, resting on her lap. "Do you remember that time you were in *West Side Story* in high school and we all ended up going on the same night?" She shook her head and ran her fingers across her eyes, the way her own father used to when he recalled something he preferred not to see. "Your dad made such a *scene* during the intermission, trying to get Dot to talk to him. Oh, it was so awful. I was just standing there thinking, *I'm never going to get over this. I'm just never going to get over this.*"

I leaned my head back, flung myself back a decade. "Yeah, I remember being backstage and wishing I were dead—"

"I think we all did," Mom interrupted, as Figleaf crawled up her sweater and settled himself on her shoulder.

More silence. A few more stars lighting up above the tree-line. "But eventually I did," she continued, almost serenely.

"Eventually you did what?"

"Eventually, I got over it," she said, smiling tenderly in my direction. "And you will too."

More stars. Wisps of an imminent moonrise over farm-land. A gouging in my chest. Visions of the man I'd just left, echoes of his voice, the infectious laughter we had shared, the passion for words, travels, warm gingerbread savoured together on cold Montreal days.

And thoughts of Mel, his dreams of retiring here, pruning apple trees, stacking firewood, gradually growing old. Before cancer crawled through his bone marrow and pulled him to his knees. Before it elicited his humility and made him the tenderest, kindest of men. A man I grew so fond of, whose sparkling-eyed smile now filled the sky.

"And you will too," I said.

My mom looked away and squinted, the moon spilling softness across her face.

III. *Sanctus*

The farm became Mel's gift to my mother, and to me. A way back to each other, and to nature—one providing passage to the other.

It started with breakfast, the sharing of early company, that vulnerable honesty of mornings. The vulnerable honesty of mourning.

We did it our own ways: she, at the piano; I, with a fountain pen. Tea by the fireplace. The Fauré Requiem. Yoga.

And at some point every day, when the last of my mother's piano students had left, we would head out the back door together with the half-blind gaggle of dogs and an alley cat, and walk.

While the land was not the same piece of music I had grown up on, it had the same key signature: hardwood forests and fields dancing free after decades of fallow release. So it was new, but familiar, including the marsh with its murky minor keys and cadences of lilies, rushes and marigolds that flowered out of darkness.

Daily, and in every weather, we padded the same path: past the garden, alongside the pond, across acres of old pasture, over the shoulder of the wetland and into the forest. Day after day, we circled its same loop, breathing its geography until it swept into me and became part of my own. Until my sorrow was held in the palms of buttercups, under the cool skirts of the cedars, and in the hollow hairs of nettle that both stung and soothed my throat.

"So was it music that brought you and Dad together, do you think?" I asked one morning as the dogs doddered around us and Figleaf followed us behind nearby trees like an elfin spy.

"I guess so. That was the main thing. But we had a lot of common interests." She paused. "And, at the beginning, at least, we had a lot of fun. We travelled, went to concerts, out with friends . . ." Her rubber boots squelched as we skirted the edge of the swamp.

"But you never suspected he was gay," I said, rather than asked.

She kicked some of the mud from her boot. "No."

It was a tired answer; I felt the heaviness in it and wished I hadn't brought it up at all.

A few steps later, she continued: "These days, you hear it everywhere: he's gay, she's gay. Every time I turn on the television it seems someone's gay, but in those days, people didn't talk about that." She shook another clump of mud from her boot. "I just thought he was selfish."

I laughed. "Selfish? What does that have to do with it?"

"Well, he *was* selfish. That was the kind of thing I thought about." She spied a red-tailed hawk and followed its flight across the sky with her eyes. Then she smiled. "But we did have a lot of fun."

I smiled back, then felt myself buckling, nauseated with grief about my own recent breakup. "We had a lot of fun too," I whispered, the tears coming so fast to my eyes that I couldn't imagine a time when I would ever be empty of them.

"I know," my mother said, her face melting into one of her great wise smiles. "Mel and I did too."

We turned and followed the path into a grove of cedars, the air suddenly cooler for their presence. At the top of the hill, the forest changed to hardwoods, maples that Mel had tapped one spring, boiling the sap down and smacking his lips proudly at the taste of his own caramelly maple syrup soaking a plate of pancakes.

"So, was Mel the reason that you and Dad didn't stay friends?" I asked.

Mom was walking ahead of me with her arms clasped behind her back. "What?" She spun around. "Is that what you thought?"

I shrugged, nodded.

We walked in silence.

Walked until the forest opened into a small wetland, where a fallen tree offered an ideal place to sit. The greyhounds wandered off on their own, the Bichons curled up on our laps. Figleaf continued his sleuthing activities elsewhere.

"Mel had trouble forgiving people who hurt other people," my mom said, looking out across the fen. "So he wasn't very fond of your dad."

That much I knew. The few times they had encountered each other, their exchanges had been civil and perfunctory at best.

"But that isn't why we weren't friends," she continued. "I remember your dad wanting me to come to these meetings he would go to with other gay guys, and later he wanted us all to do Christmas together, but he had no idea what it was like for me . . ."

A pair of red squirrels battled behind us, squawking and cursing, before chasing each other up a tree.

"For a while, at the beginning, we tried to keep things together, you know, because no one really knew what you did in this kind of situation, and we both thought it would be best for you kids if we tried to stay together. So after I found out, the deal was that he would live at home three nights a week and then go to Toronto and have his gay life there." She clasped her hands around her knee and rocked herself, dog in her lap. "But one night I remember lying in bed and hearing him walking up the driveway and then tiptoeing into the house *really* quietly, so he wouldn't wake me up. I couldn't figure out why on earth he was doing that: where was the car? did it break down? why was he walking home and being so quiet? It all just felt wrong. Well," she said, raising her eyebrows, "turns out he had stayed out so late because he had met someone and, well, you know. So he had parked the car at the top of the road and walked the rest of the way home, so I wouldn't realize how late he was getting in. That was *it* for me. I just remember thinking, *no way, I can't live like this.*" She turned to me, incredulous. "I mean, what woman in her right mind would live like that?"

I didn't move.

"So it was situations like that, and the money battles—oh, there were a whole bunch of things actually. And everything kind of soured. I know he always wanted to stay close, but quite honestly, I had no interest. I just wanted to get on with my life."

"Well, I can understand that," I said, reflecting on my own experience of feeling the same way.

We sat for a while, watching nothing in particular.

Listening.

"So it was never Mel's fault," I concluded.

My mom shook her head. "No," she whispered.

"I always thought it was. I used to blame him for that," I admitted. "If he were still here, I'd apologize."

My mother unclasped her hands, helped the dog off her lap and moved to stand. "He is still here," she said, tipping her head back and looking up into the cathedral of budding maples around us. She looked at me and smiled, her eyes trembling with tears, and started on the path back home.

I stayed seated for a while, feeling the dampness of spring all around me. Mud under my boots. The dead tree beneath me. New life greening the ground.

"Sorry, Mel," I finally whispered, looking at the sky with watery eyes. "And thanks for all of this."

IV. *Pie Jesu*

The land became a turnstile of wildflowers, one tuft of colour unfurling into the next. On good days, I would select a flower to ride in my hair as I walked, and though I never quite understood how a few wisps of colour could so brighten my way in the world, they invariably did. Gave me a florid spunk. On bad days, I would walk for hours on my own, curling up like a deer in the golden grasses, weeping until the collar of grief came loose and I could lie in a tender grace, my sadness briefly suspended in the petals that trembled around me in the breeze.

My mom played the piano, sorted through boxes, busied herself outside. We shared smiles, kind words. Took turns cooking. Salad, mostly, with a side of yogourt, or toast. Drank wine—perhaps too much. And after a time, none at all. We played Scrabble, took turns having long hot baths, enjoyed candlelight.

"So, how did you first find out Dad was gay? Did he tell you or . . . ?"

Mom reached out and played with the edge of the candle, a tear of hot wax spilling onto her finger and coating her fingertip. "I found a letter."

I knew that. She had told me once, years before, but I wanted to hear more. I wanted to know how she had *felt*. "So you just *found* it?" I probed.

She watched the wax harden on her fingertip. "He had just come back from Germany, from his sabbatical. I knew something was up, I guess, but what did I know? I remember watching him sitting in the backyard with this letter pad, fussing over something that he was writing. He seemed obsessed by it. And he was being so strange. So after he went out, I went looking for it."

She flicked the wax shavings from her fingertip onto the table and focused hard on brushing them slowly into a pile. "And it was a love letter to Tom. Do you remember that guy he shared an apartment with in Toronto when he was doing research for his book? We visited them once after your appointment with that sports doctor. Well, anyway, in this letter your dad was pleading with Tom to get back together."

I took a breath. "And you had had no idea . . ."

"No."

She stretched her arm towards the candle, touched its soft edge, dipped her fingertip in the small pool of wax.

"No," she said again, dipping her fingertips, one by one.

By one.

Finally, I asked, "So what did you do?"

She lifted her hands, five wax claws. "I went down into the basement, where he had been doing a lot of writing—remember when he used to have his office down there?—and for some reason, my eyes went straight for this box beside his desk. It was full of all kinds of stuff: gay magazines, newspaper clippings, notes to himself, letters from friends. I read through as much as I could stomach, and then I called Sally and told her I needed her to come and stay with you kids for a few days. I didn't tell her anything, but I drove up to Apsley. I had a tent and a sleeping bag, and a loaf of that black bread that never goes bad, and a couple of cans of tuna. That was it."

"So what did you do—just lie in your tent and cry?"

She closed her fingers together. "No," she said, and then smiled, wistfully. "No, I hiked up to the top of this big granite cliff overlooking the lake. It was so beautiful. I just couldn't believe how peaceful it was. I remember thinking that I should probably *do* something, but it was so nice up there, just sitting. And I kept saying, *is this ever beautiful . . . oh, is this ever beautiful . . .* Then at night, I went swimming. I'd never done that before, in the dark, no one else around . . ."

Her eyes pooled. She shifted positions, began peeling the wax from her fingertips. Pulled a tissue from her pocket and wiped her nose. "Then I came home, hired a lawyer, filed for divorce on the grounds of homosexuality, and had the papers delivered to your dad's office at the university."

We listened to Bach that night, and then my mother went to bed. I was brittle with exhaustion but couldn't sleep. Eventually I got up and lit a fire in the back room, settled into the rocking chair and stared out the long windows, imagining her swimming in that quiet, dark lake.

v. *Lux Æterna*

When I first moved to my mom's place—"the farm," although it was now a patch of wild land—I had arrived with the arrogance of an urbanite. *If I'm not surrounded by monuments to humanity, this must be the middle of nowhere.* For the first few months, I felt compelled to make regular trips to Toronto for fixes of art films, ethnic food and strong coffee. Very soon, however, my compulsions waned and the fixes became irregular, then rare. After about half a year, I unplugged altogether, tuning instead into the world around me. And to the simplicity of rural life. Cutting asparagus at the bottom of the garden for dinner, eating out on the back porch with my mother, our feet up on the table, plates on our laps, watching the colours of a sunset, laughing about something or other, or nothing.

A green heron came to live in the marsh, its ballerina toes pointing behind it as it flew. The pond became host to a beaver who carried out such extensive construction, renovation and landscaping projects with the surrounding trees that my mother and I could not help but feel sorry for his wife. I trudged through entire nations of mosquitoes, my hand across the back of my neck often bringing back a smooth wipe of blood. But my skin was harder by then, not the grated peel of flesh it had been a few months before, the bugs not so much bothersome as a fortifying challenge. Songbirds trilled and tatted the air, their canticles of invisible lace draping the trees. And on full moon nights, I would listen to the owls and dance barefoot on the grass.

• • •

In early summer, after a weekend of trying (briefly, agonizingly, unsuccessfully) to resuscitate my dead marriage, I drove back to the farm and hiked up to the forest, only to find the ground had turned white in my absence, the once-verdant floor a wash of newborn light. They were triads of porcelain, tongues of cream, hundreds of them lying open in the sleepy shade of the maples. I had never come upon such a display of trilliums before. And I had never lain among them as I did that day, finding space enough for my limbs among their leaves and resting my head on my outstretched arm. I had not intended to fall asleep, just to rest in their anodyne beauty, to shed the feel of concrete in my heels, the noise and disappointment I was wearing. But I slid into their stillness, and in the slender moment after opening my eyes, the scatter of snowy blossoms felt like gifts of grace.

That night over dinner, my mother asked if I felt I had failed.

"Because we're not getting back together, you mean?"

"Yes, well, because it didn't work out."

I stared at my plate. Lost my appetite yet again. "Yeah, I guess I do." Pushed my plate to one side. "It just feels like this *disaster*."

My mother smiled sadly. "I felt like that, too, with your dad."

"What?" I felt a faceful of lines scribble onto my face. "But there was nothing you could do—he was *gay*."

She shrugged. "It's not logical, maybe. But I remember feeling this huge sense of failure." My mother pushed her plate aside too. "And suddenly, I just sort of dropped out of everyone's lives. So many of the people we had been friends with stopped calling. I couldn't help feeling as if I was the one who had done something wrong."

"But you don't still feel that way," I said quickly.

She shook her head. "No. But it took a long time . . ."

We shifted the food around on our plates with our forks. Pesto that suddenly felt too rich to ingest. "How about a piece of toast?" I asked, bringing my half-eaten plate to the counter.

"No, thanks," Mom said. "You go ahead."

So I did, dropping a slice of black bread into the toaster and watching the coils redden slowly around it.

"So, when you were on that camping trip," I asked with my back to her. "Did you ever wish you didn't have kids? I mean, that just made everything so *complicated.*"

There was a pause.

My stomach tightened.

"That's sort of like wishing I didn't have arms," she finally said. "I mean, kids are just part of you, and you go from there. I just knew I had a problem and I had to figure out what to do."

"But you didn't regret having us?" I asked, voice like a loose string.

"No offence . . ." Mom began, and I turned around to watch her rumple her face comically. "But why would I do a dumb thing like regret the best thing I ever did?"

We both laughed. The toast popped. And suddenly I remembered her coming home from that camping trip, hearing the garage door going up and racing to see her sitting behind the wheel of the car. I would have been eleven. But I could still see her expression as she sat there. She looked so strange. As though she were made of glass. "Hi!" she had called, and then she'd looked normal again. But I had never forgotten that first look on her face. I could even recall the smell of the garage. Cementy with a tang of weed killer.

"You never feel it at the time," my mom said as Figleaf jumped up and settled onto her lap, "but it is in the most difficult moments of our lives that we do our best work as human beings. I mean, those are our opportunities to come into the depth of ourselves, to open to something greater than ourselves. And it's often someone else who pushes us there, some life circumstance, because who wants to do it on their own? It's too painful!" She smirked. "Given the chance, we'd all prefer to just keep being shallow and boring."

"Actually, I'd much rather be heartbroken than boring," I said, smirking back.

"Well, *that's* good," she continued, exaggerating relief. "To be honest, there were times when I regretted marrying your dad, or I guess that's how I felt. I don't know. I felt all kinds of things and didn't really know what they all were. I was angry. I didn't know it was possible to feel so humiliated. And I kept thinking back to the first year we were married and wishing I'd just gotten out then." She took a deep breath. "But the thing is, everything went the way it needed to go. And I have three great kids and a beautiful life . . ." She paused, turning and looking out the window towards the forest. "Just before my dad died, I remember him saying that when he looked back over his life, all he could see was how much he'd been given," she said, her voice squeezing to a whisper. "And when I do the same thing, that's exactly how I feel."

VI. *Libera Me*

Fall fanned into full colour and apples began to drop from the trees. Together my mom and I gathered up the fruits and transformed them into curried apple soup: its stock of onions and cinnamon sticks prompting choruses of lip-licking and appreciative sighs.

Geese honked away on cooling air currents and in the wake of their last V, the world quietened. Frogs sank to the depths of the pond, burying themselves under blankets of mud. Skunks denned down with their young, curling their striped tails up under their bellies and nestling into each other's musk. Darkness leaned into the edges of the days, the night a growing shroud across the shoulders of the sun.

Following a dream she had had for years, my mother headed west to an ashram in the Kootenay mountains where she would stretch, reflect and balance until spring. While she was gone, I would take over her job of passing music into small hands. We traded lives, as it were: she, the traveller, I, the holder of home. We parted by bowing to each other with our hands pressed to our hearts.

PART FOUR

The Way We See It Now

Recently, my dad told me that the Gay Fathers of Toronto group to which he had belonged when I was a child had "saved his life."

"Just being with other people who had similar feelings and experiences was so reassuring," he explained while we had tea and toast together one afternoon. "I'd read and heard stories of gay men in my situation being 'outed' and committing suicide, and for a while I used to think that anyone who followed that path and chose to lead a homosexual life would inevitably meet with tragedy." He sighed, took a bite of his toast. "But when I met Michael Lynch and found Gay Fathers, it was such a relief to be able to share our stories. And it was so wonderful being able to be affectionate with other men, just lounging and relaxing on a sofa together—oh, it was so lovely. And finally I could say, okay, I'm not crazy, it's possible to be a wonderful father and be gay, and there are all kinds of possibilities for my life, none of them easy, but there *are* possibilities."

I poured my dad some more tea and asked if he ever imagined things would have come so far in his lifetime: openly gay and lesbian people in politics, on television, equal rights legislation, legalized gay marriage.

He paused, looked pensive. "Everything is so different now. Sometimes I listen to the young guys in the swim club talking about dating or what they did over the weekend with their boyfriends, and I just marvel at how *simple* their lives are compared to the way we had to live thirty and forty years ago.

Just a few weeks ago, I mentioned something about the bath raids and several of them had never heard of them!"

Dad jumped up and scurried into the next room without saying a word, then returned waving a magazine. "But look at this," he said, passing me a gay magazine, one of the freebies found in cafés and bookstores. I flipped through quickly: pictures of bare-chested men, men in drag, short flashy articles about fashion, dating. "Nothing of any substance at all," Dad said, sitting down again. "It's like so many revolutions. Once it's over, everyone just wants to be normal. Which is fine, of course, but what concerns me is that things get taken for granted, because as we all know, rights can always be taken away again. For instance, Germany in the '20s and '30s had a flourishing homosexual culture. There were all sorts of gay bars and cabarets in Berlin, gay and lesbian newspapers . . ." He folded his arms and looked out the living room window at the quiet street. "It's important to remember that things can always swing the other way, as much as we might not want to believe that that could happen."

He suddenly lightened up. "But on the other hand, I guess I can understand people wanting to breathe a sigh of relief that the biggest battles are behind us and just getting on with the business of enjoying their lives without persecution or injustice. And there's nothing wrong with that." He laughed and threw up his arms theatrically. "In fact, what a wonderful thing it is to be able to enjoy life!"

A few months ago, my father came to spend the weekend with my son, now twelve. We had recently moved to Stratford, Ontario, a place known for its Shakespeare festival, so the two of them skipped off to a performance of *Twelfth Night*, while my partner and I headed off to a concert out of town. A few days later, I was tidying up the living room and came upon a sheet of paper in my father's unmistakable handwriting. It was a list of names. Familiar ones.

"Was Granddad teaching you all the names of the prime ministers?" I asked my son, who laughed and nodded. He hadn't heard the story of my having to recite the prime ministers in the bathtub and he seemed grateful to have been spared that part of the experience.

Despite (or perhaps because of) my earlier bathtub failure, I made an effort to develop enthusiasm for political science later in life. I even dutifully majored in the discipline at university until I realized that I only went to the lectures given by the prof for whom I had the hots, and that actually I would rather eat cat food than study politics. An odd realization, but one I came to with vociferous conviction, prompting my university roommate to look up from her Cheerios and ask, "Then who are you doing this for?" A question I was unable to answer until several years later, although it was glaringly obvious to everyone else at the time.

My father's first book, *The L-Shaped Party*, was a definitive history of the Liberal Party. My brothers and I had grown up in a Trudeaumaniacal home; we had campaigned for the local Liberal candidates, listened to endless discussions and impassioned defences of the "philosopher king" prime minister, and lived with that poster of Trudeau's silhouette in our garage and with his Christmas card hanging prominently in the front hallway all year long.

So in a strange way, Pierre Trudeau had felt like part of the family—like a distant relative who was too busy to come by the house in Peterborough but whose life and business we kept abreast of, whose face was as ubiquitous as a neighbour's and whose voice we heard in the house almost nightly.

In my early twenties, I moved to Prague and got a job teaching English to the new parliamentarians in Václav Havel's first post-revolutionary government. The parliament was full of unlikely politicians—poets and rock stars, teachers and plumbers—and my job was to meet them in the parliamentary dining room every morning and have breakfast with them in English. As far as jobs go, it was one of the most interesting (and easiest) I've ever had.

I lived in a gorgeous part of Prague near Kafka's house and the castle, which was not only a fabulous sentence to be able to include in letters home, but also a thunderously inspiring life experience. Prague was everything I had expected university to be: riveting and soul-expanding, rife with debates about art, beauty and power. Host to all-night discussions of absurdist theatre in small, dimly lit kitchens with bottles of red wine, rye bread torn from the loaf, the air filled with the spiced smoke of Indonesian cigarettes and the music of Bulgarian women's choirs. There were midnight walks along bridges whose statues whispered histories of invasions and revolutions, spire after spire after fresco after portico, nourishment in the sound of cobblestones when danced upon, in the beauty of dilapidated town squares and clock towers, and a reverence for the artistry of life itself.

It was in Prague that I began to write, curled up on a bridge looking up at the castle, on the edge of a stone fountain next to carved lounging figures, in a bustling café with gritty coffee thick on my tongue. Mostly, I wrote a journal, or letters that held phrases like *near Kafka's house*, but it was there that I also crafted my first published article, an essay about Prague's velvet revolutionary government, and a prize-winning short story that would become my first leap into the world of words.

One magnificent spring morning, in the romance of pre-Internet days, I came home from a parliamentary breakfast to find a telegram from an old friend. It read MEET ME IN CHINA and gave a long number, which I eventually connected to by telephone. Only because of the absurdity of the idea (and a recently soured tryst, I must admit), I decided to drop everything and investigate, and within a few days of unimaginably bureaucratic wanderings found that I could get there by train (via Russia, Siberia and Mongolia) for just over two hundred dollars. It seemed like too great a bargain to pass up.

A month later, just before I began my trek to Beijing, my dad, Lance and a few of their friends came to visit and to attend the famous Prague Spring Music Festival. In the weeks preceding their arrival, I spent hours lining up in queues for

locally priced tickets to symphony concerts, operas and re-
citals, finding new teachers for all of my classes and preparing
for my journey.

My dad, friends and I spent a wonderful week prancing
around—laughing, listening, eating and drinking—but Dad was
distressed at my decision to leave my job and travel across the
Soviet Union to China for no apparent reason other than that
it was an absurd thing to do. As it turned out, he had found my
parliamentary positioning even more interesting than I did and
had hoped it would lead to greater, more stable, political things.

On our last evening together, he and I had a quiet, per-
plexed dinner and then headed off to listen to Radu Lupu
performing a Mozart piano concerto with the Czech Philhar-
monic Orchestra. Because I had purchased the cheap local
tickets, our seats were not actually in the auditorium, but on
the stage *behind* the orchestra—just behind the cymbals, as I
recall. It was not the best vantage point for the concert, but it
did provide a view of the audience, which we would not otherwise have had. And so we would not have seen, as we sat down
after the intermission, the man in the third row, five seats in.

"Where?" my dad asked when I instructed him to look.
"One—two—*three*," he counted, his finger bobbing along
counting the heads. "One—two—three—four—*five*. Oh my
God, it's Pierre Trudeau!"

The concert began. We heard a good deal of percussion.
Less piano than we might have liked. But it was a wonderful
performance and my dad was over the moon, suddenly opti-
mistic about my travel plans. "I had a brainwave during the

last movement," he explained. "You see, Pierre Trudeau *also* went to China when he was in his twenties. He even wrote a book about it." I could follow the trajectory of my dad's logic without too much difficulty. *Perhaps this trip isn't a disaster after all,* I imagined him surmising. *In fact, if she follows this course, it's possible she could become prime minister!*

After the concert, we filed off the stage and down the elegant winding staircase of the concert hall. And there, at the bottom of the staircase, was the former prime minister himself, shaking hands with the many people who had recognized him. My dad grabbed my elbow and hurried me along. I protested. Told him to go ahead without me, I didn't need to meet him.

"But we must tell him you are going to China!" (A pronouncement that bewilders me still.) And so we did. Or rather, my dad did: "This is my daughter Alison. She is on her way to China, and I've just told her that you went to China when you were her age!"

Trudeau said a few friendly words and told me to tell him all about it when I got home.

The following day, Dad and I said our goodbyes. And a few days after that, I climbed aboard my train to Moscow and from there onto the Trans-Siberian Express to China. Because my train had no time of arrival—no *day* of arrival, actually—my friend and I arranged to meet under the portrait of Chairman Mao in Tiananmen Square every afternoon at two o'clock beginning six days after I left Prague.

On day eight, we were both there.

• • •

A few months after that, in the deserts of northwestern China, I sat on the back of a cart in a bustling camel market and composed a long, image-rich letter on thin rice paper. The next time I was near a post office, I mailed it off to a law office in Montreal.

Months later, a typed letter found me, almost miraculously, on a small island in Thailand, where I had gone to write up my Chinese adventures. The letter contained excerpts from Tennyson, a telephone number and three initials: *P.E.T.*

In Canada, a few weeks after that, I drew the letter from my backpack, dialed the number and announced that I was bursting with stories about China. There was jovial, strangely familiar laughter on the other end and an invitation to lunch. It was the beginning of a long-lunch-and-travel-yarn (and the occasional movie) friendship that lasted until Trudeau died ten years later.

Thanks to my dad, I suppose. Or inspired by him, at any rate.

It was about two years before I mentioned to Trudeau, while at an Indian restaurant in downtown Montreal, that I used to say his name every night in the bathtub. He raised his eyebrows, intrigued. Passed me the onion *pakoras*. I put a few on my plate and explained my father's last-one-to-stay-in-the-bath ritual when I was five. Trudeau looked puzzled, somewhat deflated. "So every night you had to recite the names of the Canadian prime ministers so that you could stay in the bath," he confirmed. I nodded. "But most of the time I just spouted a series of nonsensical syllables," I confessed. "I believe your name was the only one I ever got right."

Trudeau took a sip of beer. Gave his signature shrug. "Well, it's a dubious honour," he began seriously, smoothing out a corner of the tablecloth. Then he looked up and smirked. "But I'll take it."

I might never know the end of that sentence, but it was not mine to finish. I just had to stop writing my own version of how she should be and simply accept her as she was, frailties, disabilities and all. It didn't mean that I agreed with her choices or decisions, only that I could choose to love her in spite of them.

Which was the least I could do, I realized, considering that that was exactly what I wished she would do for my dad.

"You kids never wanted to go home at the end of the day," Dot said, laughing at the sight of some parents trying to coax their kids into gathering up their beach toys. "Your dad and I would sit there for hours while you kids played. My back would get so tanned . . ."

It was the first time she had mentioned him, and it was so casual, a sentence in passing. I turned to look at her, but she kept her eyes on the lake. Her profile was very similar to my dad's. Their mannerisms, too, were eerily identical: the way they gestured when they spoke, raised their eyebrows to punctuate a sentence, quivered their hands when they got excited.

A few french fries fell from my hands and in seconds I was surrounded by gulls rushing to gobble up the offerings and squawking their thanks. A young girl came running towards the gulls, her bare feet slapping along the wooden boardwalk until the birds lifted off into a resting sky.

The next time I looked at Dot, I could only smile at how much I loved her.

FAMILY

Dad just turned seventy-five. To celebrate, he has chosen to organize a week with the whole family in Oxford, a place pivotal and nourishing to him as a young man and one that retains tremendous meaning for him now. He has rented a large and lovely house that sleeps fourteen: he and Lance, my brothers and their wives and children. My partner and son and I will be going, of course. And so will my mother and her sister.

We leave in just over a month. The e-mails travelling back and forth at the moment are all about which one of us will bring the Scrabble board and which one the Boggle game. We're loading Gilbert and Sullivan into our iPods, checking the walking distance to the nearest pub, and the women among us are trying to figure out how to swing it so that the men do all of the cooking.

Whatever happens, we know that we can all accept and forgive one another, that the only thing of any importance now is to enjoy life together, and that the truth really does free all of us in the end.

Acknowledgements

On the second-last day of our sojourn in Oxford (the Cotswolds, actually, the glorious countryside to the north of the city), I received word that Alfred A. Knopf Canada wanted to publish this book. With my entire family around the dinner table I announced the news, and because my father is someone who virtually always has sparkling wine chilling in the refrigerator, a few minutes later we were all toasting the book's birth together.

With a glass of bubbly raised again, I would like to thank my agent, Martha Magor Webb, for her perceptive eye and her patient, genuine championing. My ebullient editor, Deirdre Molina, has believed in this book since it fell into her hands and it has been an unmitigated pleasure to work with her on finding this story's highest expression. Thank you for such delight and diligence. Profound thanks also to Louise Dennys at Knopf Canada and Marion Garner at Vintage Canada; I am honoured to be part of their library. And I am terrifically grateful to Scott Sellers for taking this book under his wing and helping it soar.

For the wildly beautiful workspaces in which I wrote sections of this book, I offer my sincerest gratitude to Nancy Rocha, Heather Morgan, Anneke & Adriaan de Monchy, Deb Gibson and Don Shipley. Each provided a version of paradise—quiet, gorgeous, sacredly private space—just when I needed it. I am also very appreciative of an Ontario Arts Council grant, as passersby who happened to witness my dance by the mailbox could attest.

Stefan Lynch and Pink Triangle Press generously gave permission for the use of Michael Lynch's writing. The excerpts from *The Globe and Mail* have been used with permission as well.

This story first came into form as a one-woman play thanks to the insufficiently heralded genius of Stuart Cox, who once saw me do an animated reading at a bookshop and was kind enough to break the news that what I was trying to do was actually called *theatre*. For his vision, direction and collaboration, I will probably never be able to thank him enough. *Gracias a* Janet Dawson and Doug Clark, who are the kind of tireless trumpeters that every artist dreams of having in their life.

Can-do-it-all Catherine Hume picked up my theatrical threads and helped me to sew them together, while continually bringing me back to the heart of the little girl in this story. I thank her for so much laughter-laced help and for sharing her dazzling creativity for a pittance. (Once, after I'd thanked her for an insight, she commented: "Hey, you're not *not* paying me for nothing, you know.")

Several friends helped write this book in that they kept me true to myself and to what was true for me. For such essential soul nourishment during this project I am particularly grateful to Trish Cannon, Citlalli Peña, Ekiwah Adler-Beléndez, Rosa Beléndez, Lourdes Álvarez and the radiant Wendy Roman. Samantha Albert was the first reader of the manuscript (with a ruler!) and her astute observations and kind suggestions were immensely helpful. And Stuart Cox and Michael Johnson were gracious enough to pass the final copy edit under their erudite and meticulous eyes.

My mother walked with me during this process with more grace than I knew a person could embody. I bow to her with the very deepest respect and gratitude. My ever-chuckling brothers were both brave and selfless in letting our lives spill open across these pages. They may always regret giving me that *Careful or you'll end up in my novel* sweatshirt for Christmas, but I hope not. My step-family has been in every way a stairway-family, in that they have brought my life to greater heights by being in it, and I am so glad history played out in such a way that we all came together. I am one of the few people in the world to have a "real" fairy stepmother and his presence in my life these last 30+ years has been a magical and hilarity-filled privilege.

Jarmo and Noah Jalava have watched me dance around in every other art form but words this last decade and they had every reason to give up hope that I would ever write another book, but somehow they did not. I thank them for such deep love and faith. And for everything else that goes into our colourful, musical, crazily gorgeous life.

It was lovely, by the way. That week in the Cotwolds with my family. I am quite certain that I have never laughed so much or so hard as I did during those seven days, nor have I ever adored my family more. Every evening, the long dining room table shook with riotous laughter, songs and general silliness, and seeing my parents so genuinely enjoying each other's company meant more to me than I ever had imagined it would. One afternoon, I watched my mother, her sister, my fairy stepmother and my father wander happily down the driveway to go sightseeing together, and the quartet of cackles that drifted back to the house felt like both the tiniest of miracles and the hugest of gifts.

Which reminds me. I've thanked everyone but my father, who has given so much to this book that his name really should stand alongside mine as co-author. "No no," he insisted. "It's your book. Use whatever you want, but you're in the driver's seat. I'll just stay in the background and try to get over my Victorian modesty." *Victorian modesty?* "I do have a *little* bit!" he giggled, looking around him. "Somewhere . . ."

From my heart, Dad, I offer you a lifetime of love and thanks. For being precisely and exquisitely who you are.

AJW
Stratford
June 2012

ALISON WEARING'S first book was the bestselling, internationally acclaimed travel memoir *Honeymoon in Purdah: An Iranian Journey*. Since then, she has dedicated herself to music, dance and theatre, and her original one-woman shows, including a stage adaptation of *Confessions of a Fairy's Daughter*, have won awards across the country. She lives in Stratford, Ontario.